Samuel Shaw

An Accurate Alphabetical Index of the Registered Entails in Scotland

From the passing of an act of parliament in the year 1685, to February 4, 1784

Samuel Shaw

An Accurate Alphabetical Index of the Registered Entails in Scotland
From the passing of an act of parliament in the year 1685, to February 4, 1784

ISBN/EAN: 9783337152598

Printed in Europe, USA, Canada, Australia, Japan

Cover: Foto ©Suzi / pixelio.de

More available books at **www.hansebooks.com**

AN ACCURATE

ALPHABETICAL INDEX

OF THE

REGISTERED ENTAILS

IN SCOTLAND,

FROM THE PASSING OF AN ACT OF PARLIAMENT
IN THE YEAR 1685, TO FEBRUARY 4. 1784.

CONTAINING

THE NUMBER OF THE ENTAIL AS IT STANDS ON RECORD;

THE VOLUME; THE FOLIO;

DATE OF THE ENTAIL; DATE OF REGISTRATION;

ENTAILERS NAMES AND THE LEADING LANDS;

WITH THE

SHIRES IN WHICH ALL THE LANDS LIE.

BY

SAMUEL SHAW,

WRITER IN EDINBURGH.

EDINBURGH:

PRINTED FOR THE COMPILER.

M DCC LXXXIV.

PREFACE.

NO man appears as a candidate for publick fa-
vour, without fome degree of anxiety; and,
humble as the tafk may be which has been perform-
ed by the Compiler of the following fheets, he is
unwilling to intrude himfelf abruptly upon the
world, and therefore begs leave to introduce his
work with a few conciliating obfervations.

It is not his intention, in this prefatory ad-
drefs, to fay any thing upon the queftion con-
cerning the advantage and difadvantage of Entails.
Upon that queftion, very different opinions have
been maintained by able writers, — fome extolling
them, as the only means of preferving ancient families, the pillars of civil fociety, — and others de-
crying them, as inconfiftent with commercial pro-
fperity. Perhaps, a middle opinion may be formed,

by

by which the propriety of Entails may be jufti-
fied, if only a certain proportion of the lands of
any country fhall be permitted to have the pri-
vilege of being fecured againft alienation, while
enough is left free to excite induftrious ambition,
which will be ftrengthened by the hope, that what
it fhall acquire may be rendered permanent.

But whatever may be the wifdom or policy of
Entails, there is no doubt that they at prefent
form an important part of the Conftitution of
Scotland ; and, therefore, it is àt leaft a matter of
very general and interefting curiofity, to know, who
are the perfons, and what are the lands to whom
perpetuity is annexed, as far as is poffible, in the
uncertain and tranfitory ftate of human affairs.----
Uncertain and tranfitory indeed they are, — of which
the Regifter of Entails itfelf affords ftriking proofs;
for we there find, that many families, which, when
the entails were made, flourifhed in the higheft
eminence, and fpread their numerous branches a-
round, have, in the courfe of a few generations,
decayed and become utterly extinct.

It

Iᴛ is not, however, as an object of curiofity only, that this Iɴᴅᴇx of Eɴᴛᴀɪʟs is offered to the
Publick. The Compiler means that it' fhould alfo
be of confiderable utility, both to proprietors of
entailed eftates, and to people in general who may
have occafion to deal with them.——To a man
whofe intentions are prudent and honeft, it is no
advantage to have a more extenfive credit than be-
longs to his fhare of property; and the confciouf-
nefs that the world is acquainted with his fituation,
is an additional motive to moderation and œcono-
my. To the infinite number of men in all depart-
ments, who may be deceived by thofe who have
the appearance of large eftates, it is furely a moft
important caution, to be informed, that thofe e-
ftates are held by a tenure, the influence of which
ccafes with the life of the poffeffor. What is now
mentioned, is fufficiently plain, and will not be re-
lifhed the worfe that it is delicately expreffed.

Sᴜᴄʜ being the purpofes which this compilation
may ferve, reafonable hopes may be entertained, that
it will meet with an indulgent reception.—— The
Compiler offers an acknowledgment of fincere gra-
titude

[viii]

titude to Mr. Campbell, the keeper of the Record of Entails, for the very obliging and liberal
manner in which that Gentleman has been pleafed
to treat him.

THE Compiler cannot flatter his vanity with ex-
pectations of the praife due to genius or abilities,
from a performance which admits of neither. But it
is a fatisfaction to think, that while thofe who af-
pire to fuch praife are often deceived, — he, whofe
fole merit confifts in attention, labour, and accuracy,
may be more certain that he has done well what
he purpofed to do. The Compiler therefore trufts,
that, as his claim is not extenfive, he will not be
difappointed in obtaining his reward.

E   R   R   A   T   U   M.

No. 641, Page 17th.——In the AUCHINLECK ENTAIL,
For *Trabroch*, read *Traboch*, and add *others*.

No.	Vol.	Fol.	Date of Tailzie	Date of Regist.	ENTAILERS NAMES and LANDS.	SHIRES.
					A.	
5	1	39	24 Jan. 1668	25 Nov. 1693	AYTOUN (Sir Andrew) of Kinglaffie, one of the Senators of the College of Juftice—Lands of *Kinglaffie*.	FIFE.
137	5	76	28 Sept 1714	22 Jan. 1715	ANDERSON (Michael) of Tufhielaw—Lands of *Tufhielaw* and *Heiflops*.	PEEBLES and ROXBURGH.
148	5	162	22 Mar. 1716	31 July 1718	AIRLY (David Earl of)—Lands of *Lentreathen*, and others.	FORFAR & PERTH.
204	6	294	6 July 1725	21 July 1725	ANDERSON (James) Merchant in Glafgow—Lands of *Rabryflon*, and others.	LANERK.
211	6	401	1 Sept 1726	16 Nov. 1726	AGNEW (Andrew) of Lochryan—Lands of *Croch*, *Cladahoufe*, *Brochloch*, and others.	WIGTOUN.
221	7	31	30 July 1708	14 Feb. 1727	ANNANDALE (Marchionefs of)—Lands and barony of *Craigiehall*.	LINLITHGOW.
224	7	57	2 Aug. 1725	25 Feb. 1727	ABERCROMBIE (Lieut. James) Lands of *Auchindearn*, entailed by Thomas Donaldfon, and lands of *Theriflon*, entailed by General Gordon of Auchintoul.	BANFF.

A

No.	Vol.	Fol.	Date of Tailzie.	Date of Regift.	ENTAILERS NAMES and LANDS.	Shires.
					A, Continued.	
295	9	20	28 Feb. & 3 Mar. 1735	15 July 1735	ABOYNE (Countefs of)—Lands of *Pittendrich*, and others.— This tailzie by James Stewart, Efq; and the Earl of Moray, &c.	ELGIN and FORRES.
322	9	303	30 Dec. 1701	5 Jan. 1740	ARGYLE (Archibald Duke of)— Earldom of *Argyle*.	ARGYLE, and others.
330	10	1	21 Nov. 1741	26 Nov. 1741	ARNOT (Sir John) of Arnot— Lands and barony of *Arnot*, and others.	FIFE.
347	10	216	21 Aug. 1740	10 Dec. 1743	ARGYLE (John Duke of)—Lands of *Royſtoun* and *Grantoun*, called *Caroline Park*.	EDINBURGH and FIFE.
358	10	356	1 June 1745	6 June 1745	ARBUTHNOT (Elizabeth) of Caterline—Town and mains of *Caterline*.	KINCARDINE.
363	10	406	26 Mar. 1745	24 July 1745	ABERDEEN (William Earl of)— Lands and barony of *Haddo*, and others.	ABERDEEN.
405	12	47	1 Nov. 1752	15 Nov. 1752	ARGYLE (Archibald Duke of)— Lands of *Ballinochaird*, and others.	ARGYLE.

No.	Vol.	Fol	Date of Tailzie.	Date of Regift.	ENTAILERS NAMES *and* LANDS.	SHIRES.
					A, *Continued.*	
406	12	57	1 Nov. 1752	25 Nov. 1752	ARGYLE (Archibald Duke of)—Lands of *Skirvenis*, and others.	ARGYLE.
423	12	259	13 Nov. 1754	6 Dec. 1754	ARGYLE (Archibald Duke of)—Lands of *Kinchregan.*	ARGYLE.
442	13	1	20 & 21 Apr. 1757.	15 June 1757	AGNEW (Sir Andrew) of Lochnaw, baronet, and Stair Agnew his fon—Lands and barony of *Lochnaw* and others.	WIGTOUN.
449	13	90	29 Dec. 1757	18 Jan. 1758	AGNEWS (Robert and John) of Sheuchan—Lands of *Sheuchan*, *Tongs*, and *Barnbarroch.*	WIGTOUN, and KIRKCUDBRIGHT.
500	14	365	28 June 176	13 July 1765	ABERDEEN (George Earl of)—Lands and baronies of *Tolquhoun*, *Logiemarr*, and others.	ABERDEEN.
546	16	56	19 June 1769	13 July 1769	AGNEW (Sir Andrew) of Lochnaw, baronet, and Stair Agnew his fon——Alteration and renunciation of the entail of *Lochnaw* and others, No. 442.	WIGTOUN.
550	16	213	8 Mar. 1770	30 June 1770	AIKMAN (William) of Broomhilton—Lands of *Rofs*, *Broomhilton*, and others.	LANERK.

No.	Vol.	Fol.	Date of Tailzie	Date of Regift.	ENTAILERS NAMES and LANDS.	SHIRES.
					A, *Continued.*	
551	16	231	10 July 1770	21 July 1770	ARNOT (Mrs. Chriſtian) of Balcormo—Lands and eſtate of *Arnot.*	FIFE.
651	19	378	30 Oct. 1777	16 Jan. 1778	ARBUTHNOT (John Viſcount of)—Lands and eſtate of *Arbuthnot,* and others.	KINCARDINE.
655	19	445	18 Feb. 1778	10 Mar. 1778	ANSTRUTHER (Sir John) of Anſtruther—Lands and barony of *Anſtruther,* and others.	FIFE.
658	19	491	2 Sept. 1778	19 Nov. 1778	ALLAN (Joſeph elder and younger) of Elſrickle—Lands of *Elſrickle,* part of *Walſtoun.*	LANERK.
670	20	168	25 Nov. 1767	10 Aug 1779	ABERCROMBIE (Captain William), with conſent of General James Abercrombie of Glaſſa, his father—Lands of *Glaſſa,* and others.	BANFF.
680	20	308	1 April 1780	28 June 1780	ABERCROMBIES (Gen. James and Captain William)—Lands of *Glaſſa.*	BANFF.

No.	Vol.	Fol.	Date of Tailzie.	Date of Regift.	ENTAILERS NAMES and LANDS.	SHIRES.
					A, Continued.	
712	21	387	20 July 1782	26 July 1782	ANDERSON (Richard) of Windygoul—Lands and eftate, of *Winterfield*, and others.	EDINBURGH.
715	21	428	23 Sept 1782	27 Nov. 1782	ABOYNE (Charles Earl of)—The earldom of *Aboyne* and others.	ABERDEEN.

B

No.	Vol.	Fol.	Date of Tailzie.	Date of Regist.	ENTAILERS NAMES and LANDS.	SHIRES.
					B.	
9	1	73	15 May 1694	5 June 1694	BIRNIE (Sir Andrew) of Saline— Lands and barony of *Corstorphine.*	EDINBURGH.
12	1	125	19 June 1688	27 July 1694	BARGANY (John, Master of)— Lordship and estate of *Bargany.*	AYR.
26	2	36	5 June 1695	8 Dec. 1696	BAIRD (Sir John) of Newbeith, one of the Senators of the College of Justice, and son—Lands and estate of *Newbeith.*	EDINBURGH.
41	2	207	5 Mar. 1700	9 July 1700	BURNET (Sir Thomas) of Leys— Lands and estate of *Leys.*	KINCARDINE.
57	3	79	12 Sept. 1701	23 June 1703	BROWN (Thomas) of Eastfield— Lands and estate of *Eastfield.*	EDINBURGH.
61	3	114	29 Sept. 1690	21 Dec. 1703	BORTHWICK (James) of Stow— Lands and estate of *Stow.*	EDINBURGH.
67	3	160	17 June 170	6 June 1704	BLANTYRE (Master of)—Lands of *Lethington,* and others, entailed by Viscount of Teviot, and Lairds of Houstoun and Pencaitland.	EDINBURGH, and DUNBARTON.

No.	Vol.	Fol.	Date of Tailzie.	Date of Regift.	ENTAILERS NAMES and LANDS.	SHIRES.
					B, *Continued.*	
71	3	200	11 July 1704	25 Nov. 1704	BURNSIDE (Andrew) of Hart-fhaw—Lands and eftate of *Hartfhaw.*	CLACKMANNAN.
76	3	229	1 Mar. 1705	2 June 1705	BLANTYRE (Walter, Lord)—Entail by Sir Andrew Ramfay of Abbotfhall, of lands of *Clints,* and others.	EDINBURGH and FIFE.
77	3	250	13 Dec. 1704	2 June 1705	BREADALBANE (John, Earl of)—Earldom of *Breadalbane.*	PERTH.
86	3	395	18 Apr. 1706	2 Jan. 1707	BALCARRAS Colin, Earl of)—Earldom of *Balcarras*, and others.	FIFE.
95	4	64	17 Oct. 1701	21 Nov. 1707	BELHAVEN (John, Lord)—Lands of *Helden, Downbeg,* and others.	EDINBURGH.
107	4	175	13 July 1704	27 June 1710	BLANTYRE (Alexander, Lord)—Lands and barony of *Blantyre,* and others.	RENFREW and LANERK.
109	4	188	8 Mar. 1708	11 July 1710	BRUCE (Sir William) of Kinrofs—Barony of *Arnot,* and others.	FIFE and KINROSS.

No.	Vol.	Fol.	Date of Tailzie.	Date of Regist.	ENTAILERS NAMES and LANDS.	SHIRES.
					B, *Continued.*	
111	4	208	14 Oct. 1706	22 Dec. 1710	BUCHANAN (John) of Carbeath—Lands of *Meikle Carbeath*, and others.	STIRLING and PERTH.
116	4	262	6 Sept. 1710	29 June 1711	BLAW (George) of Caftlehill—Lands of *Caftlehill*, and others.	EDINBURGH and PERTH.
119	4	256	5 Oct. 1711	4 Jan. 1712	BAIRD (Sir James) of Saughton-hall—Barony of *Saughtonhall*, and others.	EDINBURGH.
125	4	363	28 Feb. 1712	25 Feb. 1713	BRYMER (John) of Edrum—Lands of *Wefter Newtoun*, and others.	FIFE and BERWICK.
151	5	196	13 Oct. 1718	27 Jan. 1719	BOWIS (John) of Snadown—Lands of *Snadown*, and others.	KINCARDINE.
157	5	226	18 Apr. 1679	31 July 1719	BEAN (John) of Pitcairlie—Lands of *Slait*, and others.	INVERNESS.
171	5	378	22 June 1722	13 July 1722	BUCHANAN (John) of Torrie—Lands of *Over* and *Nether Torries*.	PERTH.
180	6	73	9 Oct. 1722	6 Feb. 1723	BARCLAY (Robert) of Urie—Lands of *Urie*, and others.	KINCARDINE.

No.	Vol.	Fol.	Date of Entail.	Date of Regift.	ENTAILERS NAMES and LANDS.	SHIRES.
					B, Continued.	
185	6	96	13 Aug. 1723	11 Dec. 1723	BROWN (Archibald) of Green-bank—Lands of *Blackfordhill*, and others.	EDINBURGH.
186	6	101	14 Dec. 1714	20 Dec. 1723	BUCCLEUGH (Duchefs of)—Lands and barony of *Branxton*, *Eckford*, *Buccleugh*, and others.	ROXBURGH, SEL-KIRRK, and PEE-BLES.
192	6	211	5 Mar. 1723	3 June 1724	BAILLIE (George) of Jervifwood—Lands and barony of *Meller-ftains*, and others.	BERWICK, LAN-ERK, ROXBURGH and SELKIRK.
203	6	290	22 Oct. 1724	22 June 1725	BUCHANAN (John) of Great-hill—Lands of *Greathill* and *Peatriggs*.	STIRLING.
208	6	308	23 Feb. 1726	24 Feb. 1726	BURDEN (James) of Fedall—The lands of *Eafter Fedall.*	PERTH.
217	6	393	22 Apr. 1707	30 July 1726	BAILLIE (William) of Laming-ton—Lands and eftate of *La-mington*, and others.	LANERK.
223	7	45	10 Nov. 1726	23 Feb. 1727	BURNET (James) of Monbod-do—Lands and Mains of *Kair*, and others, in favours of George Kinloch.	KINCARDINE.

No.	Vol.	Fol.	Date of Tailzie	Date of Regift.	ENTAILERS NAMES and LANDS.	S H I R E S.
					B, *Continued.*	
229	7	120	1 Mar. 1727	5 July 1727	BIRNIE (John) of Broomhill—Lands of *Almennefs*, and others.	KIRKCUDBRIGHT and DUMFRIES.
240	7	234	23 Mar. 1727	27 July 1728	BUCCLEUGH (Duchefs of)—Lordfhip of *Melrofe*, and others.	ROXBURGH, EDINBURGH, HADDINGTON, WICK, SELKIRK and PEEBLES.
241	7	254	23 Mar. 1727	27 July 1728	BUCCLEUGH (Duchefs of)—Lordfhip of *Muffelburgh*, and others.	EDINBURGH.
250	7	346	10 July 1729	26 Feb. 1730	BUCHANAN (John) of Greathill—Lands of *Greathill* and *Peatriggs*.	STIRLING.
251	7	351	9 Mar. 1721	8 July 1730	BALLANTINE (James) of Prieft-hope—Lands of *Prieft hope*.	SELKIRK.
26.	8	126	8 & 22 July 1731.	30 July 1731	BAILLIE (George) of Jervifwood —Lands of *Smaillholm*, and others, entailed by Captain Thomas Don.	ROXBURGH.
165	8	144	11 Dec. 1731	9 Feb. 1732	BUCCLEUGH (Anne, Duchefs of)—Lordfhip of *Melrofe*, and others.	ROXBURGH, BERWICK, LANERK, EDINBURGH, PEEBLES, and SELKIRK.

No.	Vol.	Fol.	Date of Tailzie.	Date of Regift.	ENTAILERS NAMES and LANDS.	S H I R E r.
					B, *Continued.*	
289	8	367	20June1734	9 July 1734	BLANTYRE (Robert, Lord)—Lands and eftate of *Wedderlie,* entailed by John Edgar of Wedderlie.	BERWICK.
317	9	213	4 Aug. 1737	15July1738	BAIRD (Sir John) of Newbeith—Lands of *Fuird,* and others..	EDINBURGH.
329	9	430	31Mar.1739	28Feb.1741	BURDEN (James) of Feddall—Lands of *Eafter Feddall,* and others.	PERTH.
333	10	54	2 Nov. 1741	22Dec.1741	BRACO (William, Lord)—Barony of *Braco.*	BANFF.
334	10	70	18Dec.1741	22Dec.1741	BRACO (William, Lord)—Lordfhip of *Kildrummy,* and others.	ABERDEEN.
348	10	124	10May1743	6 Jan. 1744	BARCLAY (William) younger of Balmakewan—Lands of *Morphie, Meikle Pilmour,* and others, entailed by Francis Grahame of Morphie.	KINCARDINE.
350	10	235	7 Dec..1736	15Feb.1744	BURNET (Gilbert) Commiffioner of Excife—Lands of *Caponflat,* and others,	HADDINGTON.

No.	Vol.	Fo'.	Date of Tailzie.	Date of Regift.	ENTAILERS NAMES and LANDS.	SHIRES.
					B, *Continued.*	
359	10	362	10 June & 29July1690	11 July 1745	BARBOUR (James) of Mulderg—Lands of *Mulderg.*	ROSS.
365	11	1	30July1743	6 June 1746	BARCLAY (George) of Cavil—Lands of *Cavil.*	FIFE.
375	11	163	29Sept.1747	18Nov.1747	BRACO (William, Lord)—Barony of *Braco.*	BANFF and ABERDEEN.
38:	11	177	13Apr.1731	2 Feb. 1748	BUCCLEUGH (Anne, Duchefs of)—Barony of *Eaftpark,* and *Smeaton,* and others.	ROXBURGH, EDINBURGH, and SELKIRK.
381	11	195	27June1748	30July1748	BARCLAY (James) of Balmakewan—Lands of *Ballindarg,* and others, entailed by Robert Carnegie of Ballindarg.	FORFAR.
387	11	262	11Feb. 1749	17Feb. 1749	BRACO (William, Lord)—Barony of *Glengarick,* and others.	BANFF.
389	11	334	5 May 1749	24Nov.1749	BRACO (William, Lord)—Lordfhip of *Kildrummy,* and others.	ABERDEEN, BANFF, and ELGIN & FORRES.
394	11	401	26 & 30June 1750.	28July 1750	BREADALBANE (John, Earl of)—Lands of *Eafter* and *Wefter Comries,* and others.	PERTH.

D

No.	Vol.	Fol.	Date of Tailzie.	Date of Regift.	ENTAILERS NAMES and LANDS.	SHIRES.
					B, *Continued.*	
439	12	421	6 & 10 Jan. 1755.	2 Feb. 1757	BLANTYRE (William, Lord)— *Certain parts of the Abbey and lands near the burgh of Haddington.*—This a contract of excambion betwixt Lord Blantyre and Francis Charteris of Amisfield, Efq;	EDINBURGH.
447	13	65	29 June & 2 July 1757	9 Dec. 1757	BLANTYRE (William, Lord)— *Six Acres of Land of Clerkington, and Tithes thereof*—in contract of excambion betwixt Lord Blantyre and Sir John Sinclair of Stevenfton.	EDINBURGH.
464	13	267	16 Mar. 1757	1 July 1760	BONTINE (Nicol) of Ardoch— Lands and barony of *Ardoch,* and others.	DUNBARTON.
468	13	320	17 Jan. 1758	10 Jan. 1761	BETHUNE (Henry) of Balfour —Lands and barony of *Balfour,* town and lands of *Kilrinnie,* and others.	FIFE.
482	14	108	16 Feb. 1683	11 Mar. 1763	BRUCE (Sir William) of Kinrofs —Lands and barony of *Kinrofs,* and others.	KINROSS, PERTH, and FIFE.

No.	Vol.	Fol.	Date of Tailzie.	Date of Regift.	ENTAILERS NAMES and LANDS.	S H I R E S.
					B, *Continued.*	
484	14	138	5 Oct. 1762	6 July 1763	BREADALBANE (John, Earl of) —Lands of *Ardintryve*, and others.	ARGYLE.
497	14	322	1 Mar. 1698	6 Mar. 1765	BONNAR (John) of Greigfton— Lands and eftate of *Greigfton.*	FIFE.
505	14	439	12Dec. 1763	17July 1766	BLACKWOOD (Robert) of Pitreavie—Lands and barony of *Pitreavie*, and others.	FIFE.
512	14	518	21Apr.1767	8 Aug. 1767	BREADALBANE (John, Earl of) —Parts of barony of *Strowan*, and others.	PERTH.
537	16	1	9 Dec. 1768	10Mar.1769	BREADALBANE (John, Earl of) —Lands of *Achnavade, Wefter Shean*, and others.	PERTH.
544	16	114	21Aug.1769	22Dec.1769	BRUCE (Sir Michael) of Stenhoufe—Lands of *Stenhoufe*, and others.	STIRLING.
548	16	178	6 Oct. 1769	14June1770	BRODIE (Alexander) of Lethen —Lands of *Lethen*, and others.	NAIRN, and ELGIN & FORRES.

No.	Vol.	Fol.	Date of Tailzie.	Date of Regist.	ENTAILERS NAMES and LANDS.	SHIRES.
					. B, *Continued.*	
555	16	285	20Dec. 1769	22Nov. 1770	BREBNER (James) and Francis Grant—Lands and barony of *Clatt*, and others.	ABERDEEN.
558	16	355	6 Mar. 1771	8 Mar. 1771	BREADALBANE (John, Earl of) —Lands and barony of *Strowan, Lix,* and others.	PERTH.
572	17	43	13Sept.1769	8 Aug. 1771	BLAIR (James) of Ardblair— Lands of *Ardblair* and others.	PERTH.
577	17	127	4 Jan. 1772	24Jan. 1772	BREADALBANE (John, Earl of) —Lands and estate of *Nether-Lorn* and others.	ARGYLE.
578	17	145	4 Jan. 1772	24Jan. 1772	BREADALBANE (John, Earl of) —Lands of *Aberfeldie, Beg,* and others.	PERTH.
591	17	394	13 Jan.1773	16Jan. 1773	BREADALBANE (John, Earl of) —Five pound land, of old extent, of *Murthly.*	PERTH.
619	18	385	6 Feb. 1775	23Feb. 1775	BREADALBANE (John, Earl of) —Lands of *Kilbrandon.*	ARGYLE.
620	18	406	12Aug.1769	25Feb. 1775	BANNERMAN (Sir Alexander) of Elsick—The barony of *Strachan,* and others,	KINCARDINE.

No.	Vol.	Fol.	Date of Tailzie.	Date of Regift.	ENTAILERS NAMES and LANDS.	SHIRES.
					B, *Continued.*	
628	19	1	9 Aug. 1775	9 Dec. 1775	BREADALBANE (John, Earl of) —The lands of *Stix*, and others, entailed by Menziefes elder and younger of Culdairs.	PERTH.
629	19	36	9 Aug. 1775	9 Dec. 1775	BREADALBANE (John, Earl of) —in favour of James Menzies of Culdairs, of lands of *Kenknock*, and others.	PERTH.
635	19	149	27 June 1767	6 July 1776	BUCHANAN (Mrs. Elizabeth) of Lenny—Lands and eftate of *Lenny.*	PERTH.
641	19	233	7 Aug. 1776	23 Nov. 1776	BOSWELL (Alexander) of Auchinleck, and James Bofwell, his fon—Lands and baronies of *Auchinleck* and *Trabroch.*	AYR and FIFE.
692	21	50	8 Mar. 1781	10 Mar. 1781	BOSWELL (Alexander) of Auchinleck—Declaration by him, relative to the above entail of his eftate.	AYR and FIFE.

E

No.	Vol	Fol.	Date of Tailzie.	Date of Regift.	ENTAILERS NAMES and LANDS.	SHIRES.
					B, *Continued.*	
707	21	273	2 Oct. 1779	23 Jan. 1782	BETHUNE (David) of Balfour —Lands of *Kilconquhar* and *Bellifloun.*	FIFE.
71:	21	338	5 May 1775	19 July 1782	BREADALBANE (John, Earl of) —His whole lands and earldom of *Breadalbane,* eftate of *Nether Lorn,* and fundry other lands.	PERTH and AR-GYLE.
716	21	454	26 Nov. 1774	21 Dec. 1782	BUCHANAN (Robert) of Drummakill—Lands and eftate of *Drummakill,* and others.	STIRLING and DUNBARTON.

No.	Vol.	Fol.	Date of Tailzie.	Date of Regifl.	ENTAILERS NAMES *and* LANDS.	SHIRES.
					C.	
15	1	170	1 June 1695	30 Nov. 1695	CRAWFORD (Archibald) of Auchinames—Lands and barony of *Auchinames*, and others.	RENFREW & AYR.
24	2	31	20 July 1689	18 July 1696	CARMICHAEL (Sir Daniel) of Mauldflie—Eftate of *Mauldflie*.	LANERK.
51	3	1	20 Feb. 1701	8 Jan. 1702	CLERK (Sir John) of Pennycuick—Eftate of *Pennycuick*, and others.	EDINBURGH.
68	3	181	3 April 1703	21 June 1704	CAMPBELL (Jean) of Lauriftoun—Lands of *Lauriftoun*, and others.	EDINBURGH.
80	3	307	15 July 1698	5 Jan. 1706	CROMARTY (George, Earl of)—Baronics of *Cogeach, Caftleleod*, and others.	CROMARTY.
87	3	401	4 Dec. 1706	16 Jan. 1707	COLQUHOUN (Sir Humphrey) of Lufs—Lands and barony of *Lufs*, and others.	DUNBARTON.

No.	Vol.	Fol.	Date of Entail.	Date of Regist.	ENTAILERS NAMES and LANDS.	SHIRES.
					C, *Continued*.	
98	4	114	25 July 1707	26Feb. 1708	CARRE ( ) Laird of Cavers, and Lord Jedburgh—Lands of *Eſktrees*, and others.	ROXBURGH.
108	4	183	19June171c	11July 1710	CAMPBELL (Duncan) of Culligaltro—Lands of *Culligaltro*, and others.	ARGYLE..
115	4	249	29May171c	19June1711	CUNNINGHAME (Sir Hugh) of Craigend—Lands of *Craigend*, and others.	EDINBURGH.
120	4	302	20Aug.1702	26June1712	COCHRANE (Alexander) of Barbacklaw—Lands and barony of *Barbacklaw*, and others..	LINLITHGOW.
121	4	308	8 Sept. 170.	July 171?	CRAIGIE (James) of Dumbarnie—Lands of *Dumbarnie*, and others.	PERTH.
143	5	125	6 July 1717	9 Nov. 1717	CATHCART (Sir Hugh) of Carleton—Lands of *Waterhead*, and others..	AYR..
147	5	158	31Mar.1718	26July1718	CLERK (Dougal) of Braleſkan—Lands of *Pennymore*, and others.	ARGYLE..

No.	Vol.	Fol.	Date of Tailzie.	Date of Regiſt.	ENTAILERS NAMES and LANDS.	SHIRES.
					C, *Continued.*	
155	5	212	27 Feb. 1719	28 Feb. 1719	CUNNINGHAME (Sir William) of Caprington—Lands and barony of *Caprington.*	AYR.
179	6	53	24 June 1714	22 Jan. 1723	CROMARTY (George, Earl of)—Lands and barony of *Cogcach,* and others.	ROSS & CROMARTY
181	6	77	29 Jan. 1723	21 Feb. 1723	CLAYHILLS (John) of Innergourie—Lands of *Innergourie,* and others.	Shire not mentioned.
182	6	82	26 Feb. 1723	28 Feb. 1723	CHALMERS (Margaret) Lady Brackenſide—Lands of *Brackenſide,* and others.	DUMFRIES.
187	6	123	19 May 1721	11 Jan. 1724	CRAWFORD (William) of Powmill—Town and lands of *Powmill,* and others.	KINROSS.
193	6	223	27 July 1721	11 June 1724	CHAPLINE (George) merchant in Jamaica—Lands and barony of *Collieſton,* and others.	FORFAR.
197	6	252	9 Sept. 1721	10 Dec. 1724	CALLENDAR (John) of Craigforth—Lands of *Craigforth.*	STIRLING.

E

No.	Vol.	Fol.	Date of Tailzie.	Date of Regist.	ENTAILERS NAMES *and* LANDS.	SHIRES.
					C, *Continued.*	
227	7	90	16June1726	3 June 1727	CRAWFORD (James) of New-wark—Lands of *Newwark.*	AYR.
228	7	95	25Feb. 1698	22June1727	CROMARTY (George, Earl of)—Lands of *Coigeach*, and others.	ROSS&CROMARTY
234	7	185	19Feb. 1718	7 June 1728	CORSAN (William) candlemaker in Edinburgh—*Tenement of land in Caltoun.*	EDINBURGH.
242	7	262	26Aug.1727	30July 1728	COLVILLE (Robert, Lord) of Ochiltree—Lands and barony of *Cleigh*, and others.	FIFE and KINROSS.
244	7	273	11Apr.1727	4 July 1729	CHANCELLOR (John) of Sheill-hill—Mains of *Sheillhill*, and others.	LANERK.
246	7	293	7 Nov. 1729	3 Jan. 1730	CAMPBELL (Duncan) of Larg-nahunsheon—Lands of *Larg-nahunsheon*, and others.	ARGYLE.
251	7	386	15May 1706	28July 1730	CRAWFORD (John) of Milton—Lands of *Milton, Ballennock*, and others.	LANERK.

No.	Vol.	Fol.	Date of Tailzie.	Date of Regist.	ENTAILERS NAMES and LANDS.	S H I R E t.
					C, *Continued.*	
260	8	83	6 Mar. 1693	27 Jan. 1731	CUNNINGHAME (Alexander) of Blook—Lands of *Blook*.	AYR.
288	8	364	16 Feb. 1734	28 June 1734	CATHCART (Robert) of Drumjoan—Lands of *Drumjoan*, and others.	AYR.
328	9	419	18 July 1737	20 Feb. 1741	CAMPBELL (Duncan) of Kinlochſtrevan, and Peter Campbell of Southhall—Lands and barony of *Southhall*, and others, —and lands of *Eaſter Feddal*, and others.	ARGYLE & PERTH.
339	10	122	13 Dec. 1739	26 Nov. 1742	CAMPBELL (Colin) of Blythſwood, and James Campbell his ſon—Lands of *Blythſwood*, and others.	LANERK and RENFREW.
352	10	312	14 June 1744	27 June 1744	CRAWFORD (Archibald) of Cartſburn—Lands of *Cartſburn*, and others.	RENFREW.
368	11	25	3 Aug. 1745	10 July 1746	CAMPBELL (Katharine) relict of Alexander Cunninghame of Craigends—Lands of *Craigends*.	RENFREW.

No.	Vol.	Fol.	Date of Entail.	Date of Regist.	ENTAILERS NAMES and LANDS.	SHIRES.
					C, *Continued.*	
373	11	71	31July 1662	18Feb. 1747	CRAWFORD (Sir John) of Kilbirnie—Lands and barony of *Kilbirnie,* and others.	AYR.
381	11	195	27June1748	30July 1748	CARNEGIE (Robert) of Ballindarg—Lands of *Ballindarg,*,and others.	TORFAR.
382	11	203	8 June 1733	19Nov.1748	CAMPBELL (Archibald) of Skirvane—Lands of *Over Skirvane,* and others.	ARGYLE.
401	12	14	4 July 1732	20July 1751	CAMPBELL (Colonel Peter) of Southhall—Lands and barony of *Ormadale,* and others.	ARGYLE.
409	12	84	5 Dec. 1752	3 Mar. 1753	COVINGTREE (David) of Newwark—Lands of *Warfetter,* and others.	ORKNEY.
420	12	228	8 April 1754	23July 1754	CRAIGIE (John) of Dumbarnie—Lands of *Drumeldry, New Burntoun,* and others.	FIFE.
43c	12	327	18Mar.1755	25July 1755	CAMPBELL (Archibald) of Jura, and Duncan Campbell his fon—Lands of *Ardyne, Strouan,* and others.	ARGYLE.

No.	Vol.	Fol.	Date of Tailzie.	Date of Regift.	ENTAILERS NAMES *and* LANDS.	SHIRES.
					C, *Continued.*	
439	12	421	6 & 10 Jan. 1755.	2 Feb. 1757	CHARTERIS (Francis) of Amisfield—*Parts of the Abbey and lands near the burgh of Haddington*—in contract of excambion betwixt him and Lord Blantyre.	EDINBURGH.
459	13	203	27 Feb. 1759	10 Mar. 1759	COUTTS (Alexander) of Redfield, merchant in London—*Heritable Usher to his Majesty in Scotland*—of the said office of usher.	
460	13	213	31 Oct. 1757	8 Aug. 1759	COLQUHOUN (William) of Garscadden—-Lands of *Garscadden,* and others.	DUNBARTON.
462	13	244	11 Jan. 1758	23 Feb. 1760	CAMPBELL (James) of Tofts—Lands of *Tofts,* and others.	BERWICK.
470	13	341	13 Feb. 1759 and 20 Sept. 1760.	22 Dec. 1761	COLQUHOUN (Laurence) of Hillermont—Contract betwixt him and John Campbell his son-in-law, and tailzie of lands of *Hillermont,* and others.	DUNBARTON.

No.	Vol.	Fol.	Date of Tailzie	Date of Regist.	ENTAILERS NAMES and LANDS.	SHIRE.
					C, *Continued.*	
476	14	14	5 May 1760	3 Aug. 1764	CAMPBELL (Sir Duncan) of Lochnell—Lands and estate of *Lochnell*, barony of *Kilmachrony*, and others.	ARGYLL
490	14	214	30 June 1756	9 Feb. 1764	CAMPBELL (John) of Ballevolan—Lands of *Ballevolan*, and others.	ARGYLL
494	14	279	3 Jan. 1760	19 July 1764	CLERK (Sir James) of Pennycuick—Lands and barony of *Pennycuick*, and others.	EDINBURGH
495	14	295	8 Jan. 1761	19 July 1764	CLERK (Sir James) of Pennycuick——Barony of *Lasswade*, and others.	EDINBURGH
496	14	338	7 Oct. 1765	4 Dec. 1764	CARNEGIE (Dame Elizabeth) relict of Sir James Nicolson of Nicolson—All lands and heritable subjects belonging to her at her death.	EDINBURGH
485	14		May 1759	Aug. 176	CHATTO (Lady) Christian Kerr—Lands of *Over Chatto, Smallcleughs, Hanging Shaw*, and others.	R. CLYDESDALE

No.	Vol.	Fol.	Date of Tailzie	Date of Regist.	ENTAILERS NAMES and LANDS.	SHIRES.
					C, *Continued.*	
536	15	482	1 Feb. 1769	9 Feb. 1769	COPLAND (William) of Mini-gap—Part of the lands of *Mi-nigap,* and others.	DUMFRIES.
541	16	70	7 Oct. 1763	15 July 1769	CALDWALL (Alexander) of Ne-therclofs—Lands of *Eaſter Kirk-patrick.*	DUNBARTON.
547	16	172	6 Feb. 1770	7 Mar. 1770	CUMMING (Patrick) of Barre-man—Lands and eſtate of *Clendearg* and *Barreman.*	DUNBARTON.
559	16	377	24 June 1766	8 Mar. 1771	CARNEGIE (James) of Boyfack—Lands and barony of *Boy-fack,* and others.	FORFAR.
568	17	1	27 June 1770	10 July 1771	CAMPBELL (John) of Skerring-ton—Lands and eſtate of *Sker-rington,* and others.	AYR.
579	17	161	9 Feb. 1764	6 Mar. 1772	CUNNINGHAME (John) of Bal-bougie—Lands of *Balbougie.*	FIFE.
587	17	314	27 June 1768	25 July 1772	CUMMING (George) of Altyr—Lands and barony of *Altyr.*	ELGIN and FORRES.
602	18	101	5 Jan. 1767	26 Jan. 1773	CAMPBELL (Colonel John) of Dunoon—-Lands of *Kilbride,* and others.	ARGYLE.

No.	Vol.	Fol.	Date of Tailzie.	Date of Regiſt.	ENTAILERS NAMES and LANDS.	SHIRES.
					C, *Continued.*	
632	19	88	13 June 1774	29 Feb. 1776	CUNNINGHAME (David) baker in Edinburgh——*Some Houſes and a Shop in Edinburgh.*	EDINBURGH.
645	19	313	12 Mar. 1777	2 July 1777	CHISHOLM (Alexander) of Chiſholm—*His eſtate, lying in the counties of Inverneſs and Roſs.*	INVERNESS and ROSS.
657	19	481	31 July 1776	18 Nov. 1778	CAMPBELL (James) of Treeſbank—Lands and eſtate of *Gatehead,* and others.	AYR.
690	21	18	1 Jan. 1781	19 Jan. 1781	CARRUTHERS (William) of Dormont—*Nether* or *Little Dormont,* and others.	DUMFRIES.
691	21	30	31 Oct. and 10 Nov. 1780	6 Mar. 1781	CATHCART (James) of Carbieſton—Lands and eſtate of *Pitcairly,* and others.	FIFE.
700	21	151	14 Apr. 1759	11 Aug. 1781	CRAWFURD (John) of Doonſide—*His whole lands, and other eſtates, heritable and moveable, pertaining, or that ſhould pertain to him, in property and ſuperiority, at the time of his death, wherever ſituated within Scotland.*	AYR, &c.

No.	Vol.	Fol.	Date of Tailzie.	Date of Regift.	ENTAILERS NAMES and LANDS.	SHIRES.
					C, *Continued.*	
708	21	292	4 June 1782	12June1782	CLERK (Sir James) of Penny-cuick—Lands and barony of *Pennycuick, Laſſwade,* and o-thers.	EDINBURGH and PEEBLES.
709	21	316	30Mar.1775	18July 1782	COLLOW (William) of Auchin-chain—Lands of *Auchinchain,* and others, in favours of Wil-liam Collow his grandfon, and other heirs.	DUMFRIES.
710	21	323	1 Jan. 1781	18July 1782	COLLOW (faid William) ano-ther entail—-Lands of *Over Kirkcudbright,* and others, in favours of John Collow his grandfon, and other heirs.	DUMFRIES.

H

No.	Vol.	Fol.	Date of Entail.	Date of Regist.	ENTAILERS NAMES and LANDS.	SHIRES.

D.

No.	Vol.	Fol.	Date of Entail.	Date of Regist.	ENTAILERS NAMES and LANDS.	SHIRES.
47	2	283	8 June 1693	12Feb.1701	DINGWALL (Rorie) of Cambuf-carry—Lands of *Over Cambuf-carry*, and others.	ROSS and SUTHER-LAND.
66	3	147	7 Aug. 1702	29Feb.1704	DALRYMPLE (Sir James) of Kelloch—Lands of *Coufland*, and others.	EDINBURGH.
73	3	210	22Nov.1704	25 Jan.1705	DALMAHOY (William) of Re-velrigg—Lands of *Revelrigg*, and others.	EDINBURGH.
78	3	290	10Oct. 1701	27Dec.1705	DOUGLAS (John) *alias* Camp-bell, of Mains—Lands of *Mains*, and others.	STIRLING and DUNBARTON.
81	3	338	22 Mar. & 22May 1705	27Feb.1706	DUNDAS (James) eldeft lawful fon to Sir Robert Dundas of Arniston, one of the Lords of Seffion, with confent of his faid father—Lands and eftate of *Arnifton*, and others.	EDINBURGH.
90	4	1	9 Mar. 1699	22Mar.1707	DOUGLAS (Marquis of)—Earl-dom of *Angus*, and others, in favours of the Earl of Forfar.	FORFAR, PERTH, ROXBURGH, BERWICK, LAN-ERK, and HAD-DINGTON.

No.	Vol.	Fol.	Date of Tailzie.	Date of Regift.	ENTAILERS NAMES and LANDS.	S ᴍ ɪ ᴙ ᴇ ꜱ.
					D, *Continued.*	
92	4	19	20 Mar. & 31 May 1707	5 June 1707	DALRYMPLE (Sir Hugh) of North Berwick, Lord Prefident of the Seffion, and Sir Robert his fon—Eftate of *North Berwick*, and others.	HADDINGTON.
94	4	60	3 Dec. 1705	6 Nov. 1707	DOUGLAS (Chriftian) fpoufe to Archibald Douglas of Garvald —Lands of *Cunziertown*, and others.	ROXBURGH.
97	4	95	11 Oct. 1707	13 Feb. 1708	DUNBAR (Sir William) of Hempriggs—-Lands of *Hempriggs*, and others.	CAITHNESS.
123	4	323	25 Apr. 1710	22 Jan. 1713	DUFF (William) of Braco—Lands of *Fortree*, and others.	BANFF.
124	4	343	30 Aug. 1712	18 Feb. 1713	DUNDAS (Robert) of Arniſton, one of the Lords of Seffion— Lands and eftate of *Arniſton*, and others.	EDINBURGH.
132	5	34	2 Dec. 1710	13 Nov. 1713	DICK (Sir James) of Preftonfield —Lands and barony of *Preftonfield*, and others.	EDINBURGH.

No.	Vol.	Fol.	Date of Tailzie.	Date of Regist.	ENTAILERS NAMES and LANDS.	S H I R E S.
					D, *Continued.*	
153	5	201	1 Dec. 1708 & 2 Feb. 1719	24 Feb. 1719	DALRYMPLE (Sir James) of Kelloch, and Mr. John Dalrymple—Two alterations of the tailzie of Kelloch, No. 66.	EDINBURGH.
178	6	38	6 Aug. 1711	28 Dec. 1722	DENHOLM (Sir William) of Weſtſheills—Two tailzies of the lands of *Weſtſheills*, and others.	LANERK.
190	6	170	19 Aug. 1723	25 Feb. 1724	DALZIEL (James) of Binns, and Alexander Guthrie, writer to the ſignet—Lands of *Auldcathill.*	LINLITHGOW.
198	6	161	25 Nov. 1724	22 Dec. 1724	DOUGLAS (Sir William) of Killhead—Lands of *Kennenmouth, Cumbertrees, Brydkirk,* and others.	ANNANDALE.
201	6	284	21 Sept. 1724	9 June 1725	DALRYMPLE (Sir Hugh) of North Berwick, Lord Preſident of the Seſſion—Diſcharge and declaration relative to the tailzie of his eſtate, No. 92.	HADDINGTON.
226	7	74	9 Nov. & 16 Dec. 1726	28 Feb. 1727	DALHOUSIE (William, Earl of) —Lands and barony of *Dalhouſie,* and others.	EDINBURGH.

No.	Vol.	Fol.	Date of Tailzie.	Date of Regift.	ENTAILERS NAMES and LANDS.	SHIRES.
					D, *Continued.*	
233	7	169	18Nov.1727	29Dec.1727	DOUGLAS (Sir William) of Kill-head—Lands of *Cumbertrees,* and others.	ANNANDALE.
237	7	219	11Nov.1727	13June1728	DOUGLAS (William) of Bodief-beck—Lands of *Bodiefbeck.*	DUMFRIES.
266	8	163	9Dec. 1730.	17Feb. 1732	DAVIDSON (Patrick) of Wood-mill—Lands of *Woodmill,* and others.	FIFE.
272	8	230	1April 1720	1 Dec. 1732	DICK (Sir James) of Preftonfield —Lands and barony of *Prefton-field,* and others.	EDINBURGH.
281	8	316	6 Feb. 1733	31July 1733	DICKSON (William) of Kilbucho —The *fuperiority of Hartree.*	PEEBLES.
283	8	326	15Nov.1733	17Nov.1733	DALLAS (James) of Newton—Lands of *Newton of Bothken-nar.*	STIRLING.
318	9	243	13Dec.1737	18July 1738	DICKSON (John) of Riddery—Lands of *Middle Riddery of Provan,* and others.	LANERK.

No.	Vol.	Fol.	Date of Tailzie.	Date of Regift.	ENTAILERS NAMES and LANDS.	SHIRE S.
					D, *Continued.*	
353	10	319	28 Mar. 1744	25 July 1744	DICK (John) of Pitkerro, writer in Dundee—Lands of *Pitkerro,* and others.	FORFAR.
357	10	351	14 Apr. 1739	22 Feb. 1745	DRUMMOND (James) of Comrie—Lands of *Comrie, Kirktoun,* and others.	PERTH.
377	11	120	24 July 1747	28 July 1747	DEWAR (James) of Vogrie—Lands and barony of *Vogrie,* and others.	EDINBURGH and ROXBURGH.
392	11	373	21 Aug. 1749	23 Feb. 1750	DALRYMPLE (Charles) of Langlands—Lands and eſtate of *Langlands,* and others.	AYR.
418	12	198	1 Feb. 1754	23 Feb. 1754	DUNDAS (John) of Manner—Lands of *Kingſpowhouſe;* alias *Manner,* and others.	STIRLING.
429	12	312	17 July 1713	23 July 1755	DUFF (William) of Braco—Lands of *Edin,* and others.	BANFF and ABERDEEN.
446	13	55	1 Aug. 1757	9 Aug. 1757	DICK (Mrs. Iſobel) of Grange, and Sir Andrew Lauder of Fountainhall, her huſband—Lands and eſtate of *Grange.*	EDINBURGH.

I

No.	Vol.	Fol.	Date of Tailzie.	Date of Regiſt.	ENTAILERS NAMES and LANDS.	SHIRES.
					D, Continued.	
455	13	173	25 July 1758	8 Dec. 1758	DEWAR (James) of Vogrie— Lands of *Rodis*, and others.	EDINBURGH.
475	14	1	29 Dec. 1749	22 July 1762	DUNBAR (Patrick) of Macker- more—Lands and barony of *Mackermore*, and others.	KIRKCUDBRIGHT.
501	14	388	24 Apr. 1758	20 July 1765	DRUMMOND (George) of Blair- Drummond—Lands and eſtate of *Blair-Drummond*, and others.	PERTH & BERWICK
510	14	493	12 Feb. 1767	1 Aug. 1767	DRUMMOND (John) of Logie- almond—Lands and barony of *Logiealmond*, and others.	PERTH.
526	15	315	25 May 1768	5 July 1768	DUNDAS (Sir Laurence) of Kerſe —Lands and baronies of *Kerſe*, *Ballinbreick*, earldom of *Orkney*, and others.	STIRLING, ORK- NEY, &c.
532	15	401	14 Dec. 1765	10 Aug. 1768	DUMFRIES AND STAIR (Wil- liam, Earl of)—Earldom and eſtate of *Dumfries*, and others.	AYR & WIGTOUN.
542	16	76	24 Apr. 1769	8 Aug. 1769	DUFF (William) of Muirtoun— Lands of *Muirtoun*, and others.	INVERNESS.

No.	Vol.	Fol.	Date of Tailzie.	Date of Regift.	ENTAILERS NAMES and LANDS.	SHIRES.
					D, *Continued.*	
553	16	265	6 Feb. 1764	18July 1770	DICK (Robert) late baillie of Jedburgh——Contract and tailzie between him and Robert Thomson of Eafter Fodderly, of lands of *Eafter Fodderly.*	ROXBURGH.
560	16	400	7 July 1768	9 Mar. 1771	DICKSON (James) of Ednam—Lands and barony of *Ednam,* and others.	ROXBURGH.
571	17	30	31 Oct. 1763	31July 1771	DOUGLAS (Charles) of Breckonwhat—Lands of *Breckonwhat,* and others.	DUMFRIES.
585	17	297	4 July 1761	11July 1772	DEWAR (James) of Laffody—Lands of *Nether Laffody* and *Blairathill.*	FIFE.
607	18	196	18 Aug 1773	9 Mar. 1774	DRUMMOND (Doctor Robert) Lord Archbifhop of York—Lands of *Cromlix, Innerpeffrey,* and others.	PERTH.
611	18	274	20June1774	2 July 1774	DONALDSON (James) of Thornhill—Lands of *Thornhill,* and others.	AYR.
614	18	303	13 Feb. 1769	10Aug.1774	DUNDAS (George) of Dundas, and Walter Dundas his fon—Eftate of *Dundas.*	LANERK and LINLITHGOW.

K

No.	Vol.	Fol.	Date of Tailzie.	Date of Regift.	ENTAILERS NAMES and LANDS.	S n i x' r s.
					D, *Continued.*	
616	18	331	16Jan. 1775	28Jan.1775	DOUGLAS (Sir James) ofSpringwoodpark—Lands and barony of *Longnewton*, and others.	ROXBURGH.
631	19	72	27Jan. 1776	15Feb. 1776	DICKSON (William) of Kilbucho—Eftate of *Kilbucho*, and others.	PEEBLES.
637	19	175	26Sept 1758	26July 1776	DEWAR (James) of Vogrie—Power and faculty by him, relative to the deeds of tailzie of his eftate of *Vogrie*, and others.	EDINBURGH and ROXBURGH.
659	19	510	28Feb. 1777	21Nov.1778	DUFF (Archibald) of Drummuir—Eftate of *Drummuir*, and others.	BANFF and ABERDEEN.
689	21	1	17Jan. 1778	19Jan. 1781	DOUGLAS (Doctor James) of Cavers—Lands and barony of *Cavers*, and others.	ROXBURGH.
699	21	129	12Oct. 1693	11Aug.1781	DOUGLAS (Lord William) fecond fon of William, Duke of Queenfberry, with confent of his father and brother, in contract of marriage with Jean Hay, fecond daughter of John, Earl of Tweeddale, containing tailzie of lordfhip of *Neidpath*, and others.	PEEBLES.

No.	Vol.	Fol.	Date of Tailzie.	Date of Regist.	ENTAILERS NAMES *and* LANDS.	S H I R E.
					D, *Continued.*	
714	21	417	4 Jan. 1781	10 Aug. 1782	DALRYMPLE (James) of O-rangefield, and Mrs. M'Crae-M'Quire his mother, relict of Charles Dalrymple, late of O-rangefield, and the said Charles Dalrymple —Lands and barony of *Orangefield*, formerly called *Monktoun*, and lands of *Preſt-wickſhaws*, and others.	AYR.
721	21	516	4 Mar. 1783	7 Mar. 1783	DUNCAN (James) of Tipper-malloch—Lands and eſtate of *Tippermalloch* and *Bullhill*.	PERTH.

No.	Vol.	Fol.	Date of Tailzie.	Date of Regift.	ENTAILERS NAMES and LANDS.	SHIRES.
					E.	
54	3	49	26 June 1694	4 Feb. 1703	ELLIOT (Walter) of Arkleton—Lands and eftate of *Arkleton*, and others.	ROXBURGH.
194	6	228	17 Sept. 1718	12 Nov. 1724	ELLIOT (Sir Gilbert) of Stobs—Lands and barony of *Haltrale*, and others.	ROXBURGH.
249	7	320	2 June 1725. and 14 Feb. 1729.	21 Feb. 1730	EGLINTOUNE (Alexander, Earl of)—Lands and barony of *Helingtoun*, and others—Tailzie thereof, with a difpofition by his Lordfhip relative thereto.	AYR.
292	8	405	2 & 6 Aug. 1731.	19 Dec. 1734	ERSKINE (Sir John) of Alva—Lands and barony of *Alva*.	STIRLING.
316	9	200	6 May 1738	1 July 1738	ELLIOT (William) of Wells—Lands and baronies of *Wells* and *Ormiftoun*, and others.	ROXBURGH.
331	10	8	6 Jan. 1739	10 Dec. 1741	ERSKINE (James) of Grange, and David Erfkine of Dunn—Eftate of *Marr*, in favours of Thomas, Lord Erfkine.	STIRLING, CLACK-MANNAN, and ABERDEEN.

L

No.	Vol.	Fol.	Date of Tailzie.	Date of Regist.	ENTAILERS NAMES and LANDS.	Shires.
					E, *Continued.*	
398	11	455	29 Sept. and 1 Oct. 1750	15 Nov. 1750	ERSKINES (James, David, and Thomas)—Renunciation and alteration of the above tailzie of *Marr.*	STIRLNG, CLACKMANNAN and ABERDEEN.
415	12	149	21 Aug. 1741	23 Nov. 1753	EDMONSTON (Archibald) of Duntreath—Lands and baronies of *Duntreath* and *Colquhoun,* and others.——This tailzie reduced by decree of the House of Peers.	STIRLING.
528	15	357	16 May and 19 June 1767	27 July 1768	ERSKINE (John) of Carnock, advocate—Lands and barony of *Carnock*, and others.	FIFE.
545	16	122	14 Sept. 1769	27 Jan. 1770	ELLIOT (Henry) of Harrot—Lands and estate of *Harrot*, and others.	ROXBURGH.
646	19	324	22 May 1776	14 July 1777	ELIBANK (Patrick, Lord)—Tailzie by his Lordship of his lands and estate of *Elibank, Ballincrieff*, and others.—And,	SELKIRK and EDINBURGH.
647	19	335	9 Nov. 1776	24 July 1777	Another tailzie by his Lordship, of his lands and estate of *Simprim, Fullerton,* and others.	BERWICK and PERTH.

No.	No.	Sd.	Date of Tailzie.	Date of Regist.	ENTAILERS NAMES and LANDS.	Shires.
					E, *Continued*.	
701	21	5	5 & 11 July 1761.	21 Nov. 1761	EDWINE (Lady Charlotte) *alias* Hamilton——Tailzie by Lord Loughborough, and others, her truftees, of the lands of *Mother-well*, *Eaft Greenlees*, and *Bon-hard*, in favours of the Duke of Hamilton, and others.	LANERK and LIN-LITHGOW.

i |

No.	Vol.	Fol.	Date of Tailzie	Date of Regift.	ENTAILERS NAMES and LANDS.	SHIRES.
					F.	
18	1	215	22 & 23 Jan. 1696.	20Feb. 1696	FORBES (Sir John) of Craigievar —Lands and eftate of *Craigievar.*	ABERDEEN.
19	1	228	21Feb. 1696	25Feb. 1696	FARQUHARSON (John) of Innercauld—Lands and eftate of *Innercauld,* and others.	ABERDEEN.
70	3	194	30June1703	22Nov.1704	FAIRLIE (William) of Dreghorn —Lands and [eftate of *Dreghorn,* and others.	AYR.
104	4	160	22Feb. 1707	17 Jan. 1710	FARQUHARSON (John) of Innercauld—Revocation by him of the tailzie of his lands and barony of *Kinaldie,* No. 19.	ABERDEEN.
127	4	374	20Dec.1709	31July 1713	FISHER (Andrew) of Houfebyres—Lands of *Houfebyres.*	ROXBURGH.
213	6	357	31Mar.1725	12July 1726	FELL (Robert) merchant in Glafgow—*Lands, Tenements, and others, in the town of Glafgow.*	LANERK.
225	7	66	20Jan. 1727	28Feb. 1727	FULLARTON (Thomas) of Galron—Lands of *Thorntoun,* and others.	KINCARDINE.

M

No.	Vol.	Fol.	Date of Tailzie.	Date of Regift.	ENTAILERS NAMES and LANDS.	SHIRES.
					F, *Continued.*	
238	7	225	1 May 1728	29June1728	FLETCHER (Henry) of Salton—Lands and barony of *Aberlady.*	EDINBURGH.
324	9	367	31Dec.1739	15Jan. 1740	FORRESTER (John) of Eafter Culmuir—Lands of *Eafter Culmuir.*	STIRLING.
344	10	181	4 July 1743	26July 1743	FALCONER (David, Lord) of Halkerton—Lands and barony of *Halkerton*, and others.	KINCARDINE and FORFAR.
351	10	255	13Sept.1733	21June1744	FINDLATER (Earl of) Lady Anne Ogilvie his daughter, and John, Lord Hope—Contract, containing tailzies of the eftates of *Hopetoun* and *Findlater.*	LINLITHGOW, E-DINBURGH, HADDINGTON, FIFE, and BANFF.
354	10	323	12Aug.1743	6 Dec. 1744	FORDYCE (William) of Culfh, and Jean Fordyce his fifter—Lands of *Culfh.*	ABERDEEN.
388	11	271	9 June 1749	15June1749	FINDLATER (Earl of)—Tailzie by him of his eftate of *Findlater*, in contract of marriage betwixt James, Lord Defkford, and Lady Mary Murray, daughter to the Duke of Athole.	BANFF.

No.	Vol.	Fol.	Date of Tailzie.	Date of Regift.	ENTAILERS NAMES and LANDS.	S H I R E s.
					F, *Continued.*	
390	11	352	22Nov.1749	13Feb. 1750	FINDLATER (James, Earl of) and James, Lord Defkford his fon—Tailzie in their favours, of lands of *Binwood*, by George Gordon of Buckie.	BANFF.
404	12	40	27Dec.1738	6 June 1752	FALCONER (Dame Elizabeth) *alias* Trent, relict of Sir James Falconer of Phefdo—Lands of *Balmakettle*, and others.	KINCARDINE.
411	12	108	23Mar.1753	14June1753	FERGUSSON (Mr. Adam) minifter of. Logirait—Lands of *Douny* and *Dalnakebock*.	ANGUS.
428	12	302	4 July 1755	12July 1755	FINDLATER AND SEAFIELD (James, Earl of)—Barony of *Towie Barclay*.	ABERDEEN.
461	13	232	16Apr.1759	18Jan. 1760	FARQUHAR (James) of Balmuir —Lands of *Balmuir* and *Myrefide*.	ABERDEEN.
460	13	283	23July 1760	6 Aug. 1760	FINDLATER AND SEAFIELD (James, Earl of)—Lands of *Over* and *Nether Montgrews,* and lands of *Eafter Elchies*, barony of *Rothes,* and others.	BANFF, and EL- GIN & FORRES.

No.	Vol.	Fol.	Date of Tailzie.	Date of Regist.	ENTAILERS NAMES and LANDS.	SHIRES.
					F, *Continued.*	
467	13	308	2 April and 1 Oct. 1760	21 Nov. 1760	FINDLATER AND SEAFIELD (James, Earl of)—Tailzie in his favour by Sir Ludovick Grant of Grant, of lands of *Over* and *Nether Muldaries,* *Bogbain,* and others.	ELGIN & FORRES.
471	13	361	6 May 1757	9 Mar. 1762	FIFE (William, Earl of)—Lands and estate of *Braco.*	BANFF.
472	13	390	6 May 1757	9 Mar. 1762	FIFE (said Earl of)—Earldom and estate of *Marr,* earldom of *Garrioch,* lordship of *Kildrimmie,* and others.	ELGIN, ABER-DEEN, & BANFF.
479	14	54	7 April 1759	27 Nov. 1762	FINDLATER AND SEAFIELD (James, Earl of)—Tailzie in his favours by James Ogilvie of Baldevie, of lands of *Easter* and *Wester Boynsfield,* and lands of *Bogall.*	BANFF.
483	14	121	16 & 21 Feb. 1761.	17 June 1763	FLEMING (William) of Barrochan—Lands of *Barrochan,* and others.—This tailzie reduced, by decree of the House of Peers.	RENFREW.

No.	Vol.	Fol.	Date of Tailzie.	Date of Regift.	ENTAILERS NAMES and LANDS.	SHIRES.
					F, Continued.	
486	14	160	13Sept.1763	18Nov.1763	FRASER (Captain Hugh) of Powis—Lands and heritages of Powis.	ABERDEEN.
521	15	193	5 Oct. 1767	19Feb. 1768	FINDLATER AND SEAFIELD (James, Earl of)—Contract of excambion betwixt him and James, Earl of Fife, of their lands of Montgrews, Ardneadly, and others.	BANFF.
588	17	335	2 June 1772	21Nov.1772	FORBES (Sir Arthur) of Craigievar—Lands and estate of Thainston, Beltie, and others.	ABERDEEN and KINCARDINE.
598	18	30	16Apr. 1772	7 July 1773	FARQUHAR (Alexander) of Gilmilnscroft—Lands of Gilmilnscroft, and others.	AYR.
608	18	207	16May1774	18June1774	FRASER (Simon) of Lovat—Lands and estate of Lovat.	INVERNESS.
617	18	350	2 Sept. 1770	16Feb. 1775	FULLARTON (John) of Carberry—Lands and estate of Carberry.	EDINBURGH.

N

No.	Vol.	Fol.	Date of Tailzie.	Date of Regift.	ENTAILERS NAMES and LANDS.	SHIRES.
					F, *Continued.*	
621	18	415	11 Jan. 1775	28 Feb. 1775	FRASER (Major-General Simon)—Deed of rectification of his tailzie of *Lovat.*	INVERNESS.
	19	274	19 Oct. 1776	1 Feb. 1777	Another deed of rectification by General Frafer, relative to his entail of *Lovat,* 'twixt N° 642 and 643.	INVERNESS.
630	19	64	7 July 1775	21 Dec. 1775	FRASER (William) of Balnain, writer to the fignet—Lands of *Durris,* and others.	INVERNESS.
674	20	229	22 Nov. 1669	18 Dec. 1779	FRASER (Sir Alexander) of Durris—Lands and barony of *Durris,* and others.	KINCARDINE and ABERDEEN.
675	20	244	8 Dec. 1675	18 Dec. 1779	FRASER (faid Sir Alexander)—Lands of *Kirkton of Durris,* and others.	KINCARDINE and ABERDEEN.
685	20	393	24 July 1780	8 Aug. 1780	FLETCHER (John) of Bernice—Lands and eftate of *Bernice,* and others.	ARGYLE.
693	21	53	24 May 1781	19 June 1781	FORBES (Arthur) of Culloden—Lands and barony of *Culloden, Ferintofh,* and others.	INVERNESS and NAIRN.

No.	Vol.	Fol.	Date of Tailzie.	Date of Regift.	ENTAILERS NAMES *and* LANDS.	Shires.
					F, *Continued.*	
718	21	478	28 Jan. and 1 Feb. 1783	6 Feb. 1783	FORBES (Hugh) of Schivas, with confent of Alexander Forbes his eldeft fon, of his lands and eftate of *Schivas*.	ABERDEEN.
719	21	496	5 Dec. 1782	21 Feb. 1783	FULLARTON (John) of Kilmichael—His two merk land of *Kilmichael*, and two merk land of *Whytefarland*.	BUTE.

No.	Vol.	Fol.	Date of Tailzie.	Date of Regift.	ENTAILERS NAMES and LANDS.	SHIRES.
					## G.	
37	2	159	26 Jan. 1697	2 Jan. 1700	GORDON (Sir Robert) of Gordonfton—Lands and eftate of Gordonflon.	MURRAY.
74	3	214	1 Feb. 1705	21 Feb. 1705	GRAHAME (David) late clerk of the bills—Lands of *Braco*, and others, entailed to him by contract betwixt him and the Marquis of Montrofe.	PERTH.
83	3	367	6 Sept. 1705	4 June 1706	GALBRAITH (James) of Balgair—Lands and eftate of *Balgair*.	STIRLING.
100	4	124	15 Oct. 1708	9 Feb. 1709	GLENCAIRN (William, Earl of) —Lands, lordfhip, and baronies of *Ruttifhill*, and others.	RENFREW.
130	5	18	26 Oct. 1713	10 Nov. 1713	GRIERSON (Sir Robert) of Lag —Lands of *Lag*, and others.	DUMFRIES and KIRKCUDBRIGHT.
131	5	27	11 Oct. 1711	11 Nov. 1713	GORDON (Alexander) of Auchindachy—Lands of *Auchindachy*, and others.	BANFF.
134	5	51	19 Oct. 1713	27 Feb. 1714	GORDON (Sir James) of Park— Lands and barony of *Park*.	BANFF.

O

No.	Vol.	Fol.	Date of Tailzie.	Date of Regiſt.	ENTAILERS NAMES and LANDS.	S H I R E S.
					G, Continued.	
139	5	96	2 July 1715	30 July 1715	GLASGOW (David, Earl of)— Lands and barony of Kelburn, and others.	AYR.
164	5	313	2 Oct. 1694.	28 Feb. 1721	GARTSHORE (Alexander) of that Ilk—Lands of Gartſhore, and others.	DUNBARTON.
190	6	170	19 Aug. 1723	25 Feb. 1724	GUTHRIE (Alexander) writer to the ſignet, and James Dalziel of Binns—Lands of Auldcathill.	LINLITHGOW.
205	6	297	5 June 1725	31 July 1725	GENTLES (Alexander) writer in Falkirk—Lands of Catchcleugh, and others.	STIRLING.
209	6	311	22 Oct. 1725	24 Feb. 1726	GRIERSON (Sir Robert) of Lag —Lands and barony of Lag, and others.	DUMFRIES and KIRKCUDBRIGHT.
215	6	369	6 July 1726	19 July 1726	GORDON (John) of Wardhouſe —Lands of Law, and others.	ABERDEEN.
219	6	408	9 June 1726	30 Dec. 1726	GRÆME (Thomas) of Balgowan —Lands and barony of Pit-murthlie, and others.	PERTH.

No.	Vol.	Fol.	Date of Tailzie	Date of Regift.	ENTAILERS NAMES and LANDS.	SHIRES.
					G, *Continued.*	
239	7	232	23 Oct. 1727	19 July 1728	GRAHAME (John) of Killearn—Superiority of lands of *Killearn, Ibert, Drumbeg,* and others.	STIRLING.
277	8	275	2 Aug. 1731	7 July 1733	GORDON (John) of Wardhoufe—Tailzie by the Lords Grange and Dun in his favours, of lands of *Kildrummie,* and others.	ABERDEEN.
278	8	192	23 Nov. 1730	7 July 1733	GORDON (John) of Wardhoufe—Lands of *Rochmorriells,* and others.	ABERDEEN.
284	8	332	23 Nov. 1730	17 Nov. 1733	GORDON (Charles) of Pitlurg—Lands of *Pitlurg,* and others.	BANFF.
315	9	184	22 Mar. 1731	27 June 1738	GORDON (Robert) of Hallhead—Lands of *Hallhead,* and others.	ABERDEEN.
327	9	402	28 May 1740	18 Feb. 1741	GORDON (John) of Wardhoufe—Lands of *Wardhoufe,* and others.	ABERDEEN.
348	10	224	10 May 1743	6 Jan. 1744	GRAHAME (Francis) of Morphie—Lands of *Morphie, Meikle Pilmour,* and others.	KINCARDINE.

No.	Vol.	Fol.	Date of Tailzie.	Date of Regist.	ENTAILERS NAMES and LANDS.	SHIRES.
					G, *Continued.*	
356	10	342	9 Aug. 1744	20 Feb. 1745	GRAY (Mr. John) minifter of Dollar—Lands of *Foffaquhey*, and others.	PERTH and FIFE.
383	11	213	26 Dec. 1748	3 Jan. 1749	GAVINE (John) of Whiteriggs —Lands of *Whiteriggs*, and others.	KINCARDINE.
390	11	352	22 Nov. 1749	13 Feb. 1750	GORDON (George) of Buckie— Lands of *Binwood*.	BANFF.
438	12	414	11 Mar. 1756	4 Aug. 1756	GROSETT (James) *alias* Grofett-Muirhead, of Breadiefholm— Lands of *Breadiefholm*, and others.	LANERK.
444	13	34	15 May 1756	17 June 1757	GIFFORD (Thomas) of Bufta— Tailzie, and deed relative thereto, of lands of *Bufta*, and others.	ORKNEY and ZETLAND.
445	13	48	9 July 1757	20 July 1757	GROSETT (James) *alias* Grofett-Muirhead, of Breadiefholm— Lands of *Breadiefholm*, and others.	LANERK.

No.	Vol.	Fol.	Date of Tailzie.	Date of Regift.	ENTAILERS NAMES and LANDS.	SHIRES.
					G, *Continued.*	
467	13	308	2 April and 10 Oct. 1760	21 Nov. 1760	GRANT (Sir Ludovick) of Grant, and James Grant his son—— Tailzie by him to James, Earl of Findlater and Seafield, of lands of *Over* and *Nether Muldaries, Bogbain,* and others.	ELGIN and FORRES
469	13	331	20 Dec. 1733	11 Mar. 1761	GRIERSON (Sir Robert) of Lag —Revocation by him of his tailzie and conveyance of his estate of *Lag.*	DUMFRIES and KIRKCUDBRIGHT.
493	14	256	24 Mar. 1760	17 July 1764	GRANT (William) of Prestongrange, one of the Senators of the College of Justice, and one of the Lords Commissioners of Justiciary—Lands and estate of *Preftongrange,* and others.	EDINBURGH.
511	14	508	11 May 1767	7 Aug. 1767	GORDON (Sir Robert) of Gordonston—Lands of *Gerboytas,* and *Oldmyre,* and others.	ELGIN & FORRES.
514	15	1	9 Dec. 1766	8 Dec. 1767	GALLOWAY (Alexander, Earl of)—Lands of *Glafferton,* and others, in favours of Captain Keith Stewart.	WIGTOUN.

No.	Vol.	Fol.	Date of Tailzie.	Date of Regist.	ENTAILERS NAMES *and* LANDS.	S H I R E s.
					G, *Continued.*	
516	15	27	19 Aug. 1767	24 Dec. 1767	GRIERSON (James) of Dalgonar—Lands of *Dalgonar.*	DUMFRIES.
525	15	299	23 May 1765	25 June 1768	GRAY (Captain Charles) of Carse—Lands of *Carse,* and others.	FORFAR.
527	15	351	29 Feb. 1743	19 July 1768	GORDON (James) of Knockspeck—Lands and barony of *Clatt,* and others.	ABERDEEN.
531	15	386	2 Mar. 1767	30 July 1768	GRAHAME (Nicol) of Gartmore—Lands of *Gartmore,* and others.	PERTH, DUNBARTON, LANERK, and STIRLING.
538	16	14	20 Feb. 1769	11 Mar. 1769	GROSETT-MUIRHEAD (James) of Breadiesholm——Lands of *Breadiesholm,* and others.	LANERK.
552	16	240	26 Apr. 1683	26 July 1770	GILMOUR (Sir Alexander) of Craigmillar—Lands and estate of *Craigmillar* and *Nether Libberton.*	EDINBURGH.
555	16	285	20 Dec. 1769	22 Nov. 1770	GRANT (Francis) and James Brebner, sister's sons of James Gordon of Knockspeck—Lands and barony of *Clatt,* and others.	ABERDEEN.

No.	Vol.	Fol.	Date of Tailzie.	Date of Regist.	ENTAILERS NAMES and LANDS.	SHIRES.
					G, *Continued*.	
562	16	434	5 Oct 1770.	13 June 1771	GALLOWAY (Alexander, Earl of) and John, Lord Garlies, in favours of Captain Keith Stewart—Lands and farms of *Laggan* and *Claymoddie.*—And	WIGTOUN.
563	16	434	2 & 5 Mar. & 11 April 1771.	13 June 1771	Deed of alteration relative thereto, and the entail of the lands of *Glasserton.*	WIGTOUN.
566	16	486	13 Dec. 1770	2 July 1771	GRAHAME (William) of Glenny—Lands of *Nether Glenny*, and others.	PERTH.
569	17	16	3 Sept. 1764	18 July 1771	GARDNER (John) of North Tarrie—Lands of *North Tarrie*, and	FORFAR.
570	17	30	8 June 1771	18 July 1771	Supplementary deed of entail by him relative thereto.	
576	17	114	29 Oct. 1771	17 Jan. 1772	GALLOWAY (Alexander, Earl of) and John, Lord Garlies, in favours of Captain Keith Stewart—Lands of *Meiklehills*, part of the barony of Glasserton.	WIGTOUN.
593	17	435	14 Jan. 1737	4 Mar. 1773	GRAHAME (Harry) merchant in Stromness—Lands of *Utertoun* and *Innertoun*, in Stromness, and others.	ORKNEY.

No.	Vol.	Fol.	Date of Tailzie.	Date of Regift.	ENTAILERS NAMES and LANDS.	SHIRES.
					G, *Continued.*	
601	18	96	23July.1772	17Dec.1773	GIBB (William) of Templebog-wood—-Lands of *Templebog-wood*.	AYR.
652	19	402	15Aug.1776	23Jan. 1778	GORDON (Alexander) of Cul-vennan—Lands and eſtate of *Greenlaw*, and others.	KIRKCUDBRIGHT.
688	20	419	8 May 1780	23Dec.1780	GRANT (Mrs. Grizel) *alias* Mil-ler, and others, truſtees of Wil-liam Grant of Preſtongrange, in favours of Janet Grant, now Counteſs of Hyndford, *&c.*—Lands of *Lethenhope*, and o-thers.	PEEBLES, EDIN-BURGH, and BER-WICK.
694	21	82	22Apr.1780	29June1781	GIBSON (Sir John) of Pentland—Lands and barony of *Pent-land*, and others.—And	EDINBURGH.
694	21	94		29June1781	Declaration by him relative to ſaid deed of tailzie.	
695	21	96	2 Dec. 1773	14July 1781	GIBSON (William) of Bridge-toun—Lands of *Craigbill* and *Bridgetoun*, and others, and lands of *Little Fithie*, in fa-vours of his daughter and William Orr, her ſon.	KINCARDINE and FORFAR.

No.	Vo!	Fo!	Date of Tailzi.	Date of Regifl.	ENTAILERS NAMES and LANDS.	SUIRES.
					G, *Continued.*	
692	21	117	5 Mar. 1781	14July 1781	GIBSON (faid William)—Lands of *Wefter Pitgarvie*, and others, in favour of his faid daughter and her fon.	KINCARDINE.
703	21	188	11Sept. 1781	30Nov.1781	GILLESPIE (Doctor John) of Kirktoun—Eftate of *Kirktoun*, and others.	FIFE.

Q

No.	Vol.	Fol.	Date of Tailzie.	Date of Regift.	ENTAILERS NAMES and LANDS.	S H I R E S.
					H.	
10	1	81	3 Oct. 1693	4 July 1694	HAMILTON (William, Duke of) —The dukedom of *Hamilton*.	LANERK.
25	2	33	16 Apr. 1674	4 Dec. 1696	HOPE (John) of Hopetoun—*All and sundry his Lands, Estates, and Heritages, wherever they ly.*	Shire not mentioned.
28	2	48	23 Oct. 1695	25 Feb. 1697	HOSPITAL (Trinity)—Mortification and tailzie in favour of that hospital by Mr. James A-lexander—-Lands of *Redhall*, and others.	DUMFRIES.
35	2	125	10 Jan. 1673	23 Feb. 1699	HEPBURNS (Barbara, Anne, and Isobel) heirs-portioners of Blackcastle—-Lands and estate of *Blackcastle*, and others.	EDINBURGH and BERWICK.
75	3	226	8 Mar. 1678	1 June 1705	HALKET (Sir Charles) of Pitfirran—-Lands and estate of *Pitfirran*.	FIFE.
102	4	141	10 June 1709	10 June 1709	HAMILTON (Thomas) of Falahall—Lands of *Falahall*, and others.	EDINBURGH.

No.	Vol.	Fol.	Date of Tailzie.	Date of Regist.	ENTAILERS NAMES and LANDS.	SHIRES.
					H, Continued.	
128	4	387	30 Aug 1709	4 Nov. 1713	HUNTER (Andrew) of Dod—Lands and barony of *Dod*, and others.	FORFAR.
129	4	399	19 Jan. 1713	4 Nov. 1713	HUNTER (said Andrew) of Dod—Some acres called *Eyving Hills*, and other houses.	FORFAR.
140	5	108	1 Feb. 1716	9 Feb. 1716	HERON (Andrew) of Bargally—Lands of *Bargally*, *Barhouse*, and others.	KIRKCUDBRIGHT.
145	5	143	Feb. 1718.	28 Feb. 1718	HERON (said Andrew)—Rental referred to in his entail of *Bargally*, and others.	KIRKCUDBRIGHT.
159	5	243	22 May 1718	23 Jan. 1720	HOPE-BRUCE (Sir Thomas) of Kinross—Estate of *Craighall*.	Shire not mentioned.
175	6	1	10 Sept. 1722	16 Nov. 1722	HOPETOUN (Charles, Earl of)—Lands and barony of *Crawfordmuir*, and others.	LANERK and LINLITHGOW.
183	6	87	29 Oct. 1723	2 Nov. 1723	HALIDAY (Robert) of Tillibole—Lands of *Tillibole*, and others.	KINROSS.

No.	Vol.	Fol.	Date of Tailzie.	Date of Regift.	ENTAILERS NAMES and LANDS.	SHIRES.
					H, *Continued.*	
191	6	179	13Feb. 1723	26Feb. 1724	HOME (Sir Patrick) of Renton— Lands of *Lumſdaine,* and others.	BERWICK and EDINBURGH.
230	7	128	24Nov.1726	18July 1727	HAMILTON (Major Gavin) of Raploch—-Lands of *Raploch,* and others.	LANERK.
279	8	301	24July 1733	25July 1733	HORN (John) of that Ilk—Lands of *Weſthall,* and others.	ABERDEEN.
309	9	106	23May 1734	24Dec.1736	HANNAY (Anna) of Kingſmuir —Lands of *Kingſmuir.*	FIFE.
351	10	255	13Sept.1733	21June1744	HOPE (Lord John)—Contract of marriage betwixt him and Lady Anne Ogilvie, daughter to the Earl of Findlater, containing tailzie of the eſtates of *Hopetoun* and *Findlater.*	LINLITHGOW, E-DINBURGH, HADDINGTON, FIFE, and BANFF.
355	10	330	24Oct. 1738	20Jan. 1745	HOME (Ninian) of Billie—Lands of *Heughhead,* and others.	BERWICK.
366	11	8	18Feb. 1745	14June1746	HAMILTON (Archibald, Lord) one of the Lords of the Admiralty—Lands of *Riccartoun,* and others.	LINLITHGOW.

R

No.	Vol.	Fol.	Date of Tailzie.	Date of Regist.	ENTAILERS NAMES and LANDS.	SHIRE.
					H,' *Continued.*	
369	11	31	3 Nov. 1746	11 Nov. 1746	HOPE (Charles) of Craigiehall—Tailzie by Robert Myrton to him of the barony of *Lenny*.	EDINBURGH.
396	11	435	12 Feb. 1750	14 Nov. 1750	HOPETOUN (John, Earl of)—Lands of *Lawgreen, Greenridge*, and others.	LINLITHGOW.
403	12	26	9 June 1748	22 Feb. 1752	HAY (Sir Robert) of Linplum—Lands and barony of *Linplum*, and *Baro*, and all his other lands.	No shire mentioned.
412	12	111	11 Apr. 1752	16 Nov. 1753	HOPETOUN (John, Earl of)—Lands and barony of *Bathgate*, and others.	EDINBURGH, LINLITHGOW, and DUMFRIES.
413	12	122	11 Apr. 1752	16 Nov. 1753	HOPETOUN (said John, Earl of)—Lands and barony of *Ormiston*, and others.	EDINBURGH.
414	12	133	11 Apr. 1752	16 Nov. 1753	HOPETOUN (said John, Earl of)—Lands and barony of *Luffness*, and others.	EDINBURGH and FIFE.
416	12	167	26 Jan. 1740	20 Dec. 1753	HOME (Ninian) of Billie—Lands of *Nunmeadow* and *Nunbutts*, and others.	BERWICK.

No.	Vol.	Fol.	Date of Tailzie.	Date of Regist.	ENTAILERS NAMES and LANDS.	SHIRES.
					H, *Continued.*	
424	12	268	11 June 1740	14 Feb. 1755	HENDERSON (James) of Earlshall—Lands of *Earlshall*, and others.	FIFE.
431	12	336	19 July 1755	25 July 1755	HAMILTON (Sir Hugh) of Rosehall—Lands and barony of *Medrox*, and others.	LANERK, EDINBURGH, and RENFREW.
433	12	367	14 July 1746	13 Nov. 1755	HAMILTON (Lady Mary) relict of Lord Basil Hamilton—Lands of *Baldoon*, and others.	WIGTOUN.
451	13	118	2 Mar. 1758	7 Mar. 1758	HOPETOUN (John, Earl of)—Lands and barony of *Bathgate*, and others.	LINLITHGOW and EDINBURGH.
452	13	133	2 Mar. 1758	7 Mar. 1758	HOPETOUN (said John, Earl of)—Lands and barony of *Rankeilor*.	FIFE.
453	13	148	2 Mar. 1758	7 Mar. 1758	HOPETOUN (said John, Earl of)—Lands and barony of *Luffness* and *Waughton*.	EDINBURGH.
473	13	425	10 June 1709	5 Mar. 1762	HAMILTON (Colonel Thomas) of Falahall—Lands and estate of *Fala*, and others.	ROXBURGH and EDINBURGH.

No.	Vol.	Fol.	Date of Tailzie.	Date of Regift.	ENTAILERS NAMES and LANDS.	SHIRES.
					H, *Continued.*	
474	13	434	27Oct.1757	22June1762	HYNDFORD (John, Earl of)— *His Lands, Baronies, and Eſtate, lying within the ſhires of*	LANERK and AYR.
491	14	232	31May1764	26June1764	HOPETOUN (John, Earl of)— Lands and eſtate of *Craigtoun,* and others.	LINLITHGOW.
518	15	52	10Sept.1762	21Jan. 1768	HYNDFORD (John, Earl of)— *His whole entailed Eſtate, Lands and Heritages*—And	LANERK and AYR.
518	15	70	24Dec.1764	21Jan. 1768	Deed of alteration relative thereto by his Lordſhip.	
523	15	268	9 June 1766	16June1768	HALDANE (Robert) of Gleneagles—Lands and baronies of *Gleneagles* and *Haldane,* and others.	PERTH, DUNBARTON, and STIRLING.
554	16	275	13Feb. 1770	8 Aug. 1770	HALCRO (Doctor Hugh) of Coubiſta—Iſland and lands of *Cava,* and others.	ORKNEY.
565	16	468	22Feb. 1771	22June1771	HAY (William) of Thomaſtoun—Lands of *Eaſter* and *Middle Thomaſtouns.*	STIRLING.

No.	Vol.	Fol.	Date of Tailzie.	Date of Regift.	ENTAILERS NAMES and LANDS.	SHIRES.
					H, *Continued.*	
580	17	176	29Apr.1772	19June1772	HALKERSTON (Helenus) of Rathillet, and John Swete of Pleafantfield, of the kingdom of Ireland, containing tailzie of the lands and eftate of *Rathillet.*	FIFE.
590	17	364	3 Mar. 1770	10Dec.1772	HOG (Roger) of Newlifton— Lands and eftate of *Nether Newlifton,* and others.	LINLITHGOW.
592	17	409	31Jan. 1747	17Feb. 1773	HAMILTON (Alexander) of Pencaitland—Lands and barony of *Pencaitland, Dechmont, Saltcoats,* and others.	HADDINGTON.
594	17	448	13May 1763	25June1773	HAMILTON (Robert) of Bourtriehill—-Lands and eftate of *Pearfton, Blair, Dreghorn,* and others.	AYR.
595	17	470	31Dec.1768	25June1773	HAMILTON (faid Robert)— Lands and eftate of *Barhill, Nether* and *Over Broomlands,* and others.	AYR.
597	18	13	11June1773	3 July 1773	HAMILTONS (Katharine and Mary) daughters of John Hamilton of Bardowie—of their parts of the lands of *Bardowie,* and others.	STIRLING.

No.	Vol.	Fol.	Date of Tailzie	Date of Regist.	ENTAILERS NAMES and LANDS.	SHIRES.
					H, *Continued.*	
600	18	70	27 July 1773	11 Aug. 1773	HOPETOUN (John, Earl of)— Lands of *Craigtoun, Ballincrieff, Kilpunt,* and others, in excambion of other lands in the old tailzie of *Hopetoun.*	EDINBURGH and FIFE.
603	18	115	13 Aug. 1773	5 Mar. 1774	HOPETOUN (John, Earl of)— Lands and barony of *Ormiston, Belsis,* and others.—And	
604	18	145	13 Aug. 1773	5 Mar. 1774	HOPETOUN (said John, Earl of) —Deed relative to the immediate preceding tailzie, empowering the heirs to sell certain parts of the lands.	HADDINGTON, LINLITHGOW, EDINBURGH, DUMFRIES, and FIFE.
605	18	150	10 Aug. 1773	5 Mar. 1774	HOPETOUN (said John, Earl of) —Lands and baronies of *Craighall, Kinninmonth,* and others.	FIFE.
606	18	173	10 Aug. 1773	5 Mar. 1774	HOPETOUN (said John, Earl of) —Baronies of *Luffness, Waughton,* and others.	HADDINGTON.
626	18	487	Date wanting.	21 Nov. 1775	HAY (John) of Morton—The estate of *Morton.*	FIFE.

No.	Vol.	Fol.	Date of Tailzie.	Date of Regift.	ENTAILERS NAMES and LANDS.	SHIRES.
					H, *Continued.*	
627	18	494	9 Feb. 1768	7 Dec. 1775	HOME-STEWART (David) of Argaty—Lands and barony of *Argaty*, and others.	PERTH.
636	19	157	16 Aug. 1775	10 July 1776	HAY (Andrew) of Rannas—Lands and eſtate of *Rannas*, and others.	BANFF.
642	19	265	14 Mar. 1775	17 Jan. 1777	HAMILTON (Major Charles)—Lands and eſtate of *Fairholm*.	LANERK.
653	19	418	23 Sept. 1775	23 Jan. 1778	HOUSTOUN (Andrew) of Jordanhill—Lands and eſtate of *Jordanhill*, and others—And Deed of revocation of the ſaid entail, as to certain clauſes.	RENFREW and LANERK.
681	20	323	13 April, 22 May, and 10 June 1780	14 July 1780	HOME (Alexander, Earl of) and William, Lord Dunglaſs his ſon, and their truſtees—The barony of *Home*, lordſhip of *Coldingham*, lands of *Hirſell*, and others.	BERWICK and ROXBURGH.
683	20	363	10 Jan. 1775	28 July 1780	HAY (John) of Beltoun—Lands and eſtate of *Beltoun* and *Beltoundod*, with the pertinents.	HADDINGTON.

٣

[73]

No.	Vol.	Fol.	Date of Tailzie.	Date of Regist.	ENTAILERS NAMES and LANDS.	S H I R E S.
					I.	
1	1	1	4 Sept. 1687	31 July 1688	IRVINE (Alexander) of Murtle—Lands and barony of *Drum*.	ABERDEEN.
44	2	229	18 Dec. 1699	30 July 1700	JOHNSTON (John) of Newplace—Lands of *Craig*, and others, entailed to him by Thomas Shand of Craig.	ABERDEEN.
56	3	75	6 Mar. 1697	10 June 1703	JARDINE (Sir Alexander) of Applegirth—-Lands and barony of *Applegirth, and all other his Lands and Heritages.*	No shire mentioned.
154	5	207	12 Feb. 1719	27 Feb. 1719	INGLIS (Alexander) of Murdieston—Lands and estate of *Murdieston*, and others.	LANERK.
262	8	96	18 Aug. 1712	25 Feb. 1731	JOHNSTON (Robert) of Kelton—Lands and estate of *Thrive-Grange, Kelton*, and others.	KIRKCUDBRIGHT.
312	9	128	25 Mar. 1727	30 July 1737	IRVINE (John) of Drum—Tailzie by Alexander Tytler, writer in Edinburgh, William, Earl of Aberdeen, and Patrick Duff of Premnay, in his favours, of the estate of *Drum*.	ABERDEEN and KINCARDINE.

T

No.	Vol.	Fol.	Date of Tailzie.	Date of Regist.	ENTAILERS NAMES and LANDS.	SHIRES.
					I, *Continued.*	
320	9	270	23 Feb. and 18May 1739	15 June 1739	JUSTICE (James) his fpoufe, and fon—Two tailzies in their favours, by Thomas Matthie and James Watterftoun—Lands of *Ugfton* and *Over Houden.*	BERWICK.
336	10	104	17 Mar. 1741	18 June 1742	JOHNSTON (Alexander) of Straiton—Lands and eftate of *Straiton,* and others.	EDINBURGH.
343	10	176	30 June 1743	10 July 1743	IRVINE (Alexander) of Saphock —Lands of *Saphock,* and others. *Nota.* Revocation of this tailzie, regiftered in the books of Seffion, (J. K.) 10th June 1745.	ABERDEEN.
529	15	370	28 July 1768	30 July 1768	INNES (John) of Dunkinty—Lands and eftate of *Dunkinty,* and others.	ELGIN & FORRES.
622	18	418	19 Dec. 1765	7 Mar. 1775	IRVINE (William) of Bonefhaw —Lands and eftate of *Bonefhaw.*	DUMFRIES.

No.	Vol.	Fol.	Date of Tailzie.	Date of Regift.	ENTAILERS NAMES and LANDS.	SHIRES.
					I, Continued.	
582	20	348	20June1780	22July 1780	JOHNSTON (James) of Sands— Lands and estate of *Sands*, and others.	PERTH.
584	20	38c	18Sept.1779	4 Aug. 1780	JOHNSTON (William) of Lock-erbie—Lands and estate of *Lockerbie*.	DUMFRIES.

No.	Vol.	Fol.	Date of Tailzie.	Date of Regift.	ENTAILERS NAMES and LANDS.	SHIRE t.
					K.	
7	1	46	21 Aug. 1679	27 Feb. 1694	KINNAIRD (Lord George)—-Lands and eftate of *Kinnaird*.	PERTH.
20	1	236	3 April 1695	27 Feb. 1696	KINTORE.(John, Earl of)—Earldom and eflate of *Kintore*.	ABERDEEN.
27	2	44	16 Sept. 1675	1 Jan. 1697	KENNEDY (John) of Kirkmichael—Lands of *Kirkmichael*.	AYR.
32	2	89	23 & 27 Feb. 1694.	14 July 1698	KINTORE (John, Earl of)—The earldom of *Kintore*.	ABERDEEN.
72	3	205	13 Dec. 1688	21 Dec. 1704	KENNEDY (Quintine) of Drummellan—Lands of *Drummellan*, and others.	AYR.
99	4	123	8 June 1708	15 June 1708	KINTORE (John, Earl of)—Eik to the tailzie of *Kintore*.	ABERDEEN.
106	4	173	7 Jan. 1710	15 Feb. 1710	KINTORE (Earl of)—-Another eik to the tailzie of *Kintore* by his Lordfhip and Lord Inverurie.	ABERDEEN.
133	5	44	23 June 1713	3 Dec. 1713	KERR (Andrew) of Morrifton—Lands ~~of~~ *Morrifton*, and others.	BERWICK.

U

No.	Vol.	Fol.	Date of Tailzie	Date of Regift.	ENTAILERS NAMES and LANDS.	SHIRES.
					K, *Continued.*	
2co	6	281	27 Apr. 1724	27 Feb. 1725	KERR (Andrew) of Lochinches —Lands of *Lochinches* or *Hofe-law.*	ROXBURGH.
269	8	194	29 May 1732	22 June 1732	KEIR (William) of Kinmonth— Lands of *Kinmonth*, and others.	PERTH.
286	8	351	26 June 1730	6 Dec. 1733	KERR (Andrew) of Morrifton— Lands of *Morrifton*, and others.	BERWICK.
3co	9	28	25 Apr. 1735	30 July 1735	KINLOCH (George) of Kair— Lands of *Fallfide* and *Brecks.*— Tailzie thereof in his favour by John Fullerton.	KINCARDINE.
304	9	52	6 May 1736	22 June 1736	KERR (William) of Abbotrule— Lands of *Abbotrule*, and others.	ROXBURGH.
326	9	394	11 Aug. 1740	31 Jan. 1741	KIRKPATRICK (Sir Thomas) of Clofeburn—Lands and eftate of *Brigburgh*, and others.	DUMFRIES.
371	11	61	3 Feb. 1746	11 Dec. 1746	KERR (John) of Kippielaw— Lands and eftate of *Kippielaw*, and others.	ROXBURGH.

No.	Vol.	Fol.	Date of Tailzie.	Date of Regift.	ENTAILERS NAMES and LANDS.	SHIRES.
					K, *Continued.*	
374	11	80	12 Jan. 1747	10 July 1747	KINLOCH (Sir Francis) of Gilmerton—Lands and estate of *Gilmerton*, and others—And Deed of alteration relative thereto.	EDINBURGH.
407	12	71	3 Dec. 1743	9 Feb. 1753	KIRKPATRICK (Sir Thomas) of Clofeburn—Deed of alteration of the tailzie of his estate, N° 326.	DUMFRIES.
421	12	239	13 Aug. 1746	6 Aug. 1754	KENNEDY (Thomas) of Denure—Lands and barony of *Denure*, and others.	AYR.
485	14	150	17 May 1759	2 Aug. 1763	KERR (Chriftian) Lady Chatto—Lands of *Over Chatto*, *Smallcleughs*, *Hanging fhaw*, and others.	ROXBURGH.
499	14	343	27 Apr. 1764	21 June 1765	KELSO (Mrs. Mary) *alias* M'Gill, and Jean Kelfo her fifter—Lands and estate of *Dankeith*, and others.	AYR.
609	18	234	14 Mar. 1774	18 June 1774	KINNOUL (Thomas, Earl of)—Lands and barony of *Rattray*.	PERTH.

No.	Vol.	Fól.	Date of Tailzie.	Date of Regift.	ENTAILERS NAMES and LANDS.	SHIRES.
					K, Continued.	
610	18	244	14Mar.1774	18June1774	KINNOUL (faid Thomas, Earl of)—-Lands and barony of *Balhoufie.*	PERTH.
612	18	283	18June1774	8 July 1774	KNIGHT (Captain John) of Jordinfton—Lands and eftate of *Jordinfton.*	PERTH.
638	19	180	6Nov. 1776	19Nov.1776	KENNEDY (David) of Craig—Lands and eftate of *Craig,* and others.	AYR.
654	19	435	22Apr.1777	28Jan. 1778	KING (William) of Formakin—Lands of *Formakin,* alias *Millbank.*	RENFREW.
671	20	183	28July 1779	10Aug.1779	KINNOUL (Thomas, Earl of)—Lands and barony of *Balhoufie, Rattray,* and others.	PERTH.

No.	Vol.	Fol.	Date of Tailzie	Date of Regift.	ENTAILERS NAMES and LANDS.	SHIRES.
					L.	
8	1	64	22Feb. 1693	27Feb. 1694	LOCKHART (Cromwell) of Lee —Lands and eftate of *Lee.*	LANERK.
22	2	8	29Nov.1695	30July 1696	LOCKHART (Sir John) of Caftle-hill—Lands and eftate of *Caftle-hill.*	LANERK.
23	2	27	No date.	2 Dec. 1696	LAUDER (John) of Fountain-hall—Lands and eftate of *Foun-tainhall.*	No fhire mentioned.
31	2	80	8 Nov. 1692	25Feb. 1698	LESLIE (Patrick, Count) of Bal-quhain—Lands and eftate of *Balquhain.*	ABERDEEN.
36	2	137	17May 1682	25July 1699	LITTLE (William) of Libber-toun—Lands and eftate of *Lib-bertoun.*	EDINBURGH.
43	2	224	13July 1700	30July 1700	LESLIE (Patrick, Count) of Bal-quhain—Lands and eftate of *Balquhain.*	ABERDEEN.
53	3	36	17Dec.1702	26Dec.1702	LIVINGSTON (Alexander) of Badlormie—Lands and eftate of *Badlormie.*	LINLITHGOW.

X

No.	Vol.	Fol.	Date of Tailzie.	Date of Regist.	ENTAILERS NAMES and LANDS.	SHIRES.
					L, *Continued.*	
55	3	56	31 Aug. 1702	12 Feb. 1703	LAUDERDALE (John, Earl of) —-Lordſhip and barony of *Thirleſtane,* and others.	EDINBURGH, BER-WICK, and REN-FREW.
122	4	316	12 July 1712	19 July 1712	LOCKHART (George) of Carn-wath—Lands and barony of *Carnwath,* and others.	LANERK.
158	5	240	8 Mar. 1705	10 Dec. 1719	LIVINGSTON (James) of Weſt-quarter—Lands and eſtate of *Weſtquarter,* and others, entail-ed by the Counteſs of Findla-ter, with conſent of the Earl her huſband.	STIRLING.
176	6	21	31 Oct. 1721	28 Nov. 1722	LOCKHART (George) of Carn-wath—Lands and barony of *Carnwath,* and others.	LANERK and DUM-FRIES.
232	7	157	28 June 1727	12 Dec. 1727	LAURIE (Walter) of Redcaſtle—Lands of *Redcaſtle,* and others.	KIRKCUDBRIGHT and WIGTOUN.
236	7	196	23 Feb. 1714	7 June 1728	LOCKHART (Dame Martha) ſpouſe to Sir John Sinclair of Stevenſton—Lands and eſtate of *Caſtlehill.*	LANERK.

No.	Vol.	Fol.	Date of Tailzie.	Date of Regist.	ENTAILERS NAMES and LANDS.	SHIRES.
					L, *Continued.*	
253	7	366	24 July 1730	25 July 1730	LESLIE (James) of Tullich—Lands and eftate of *Davoch,* and lands of *Rananvie.*	BANFF.
282	8	318	20 Oct. 1733	17 Nov. 1733	LESLIES (John and Alexander) of Warthill—Town and lands of *Cuffiftoun, Warthill,* and others.	ABERDEEN.
285	8	339	20 Nov. 1733	23 Nov. 1733	LAURIE (Walter) of Redcaftle—Lands and eftate of *Bargattin,* and others.	KIRKCUDBRIGHT.
302	9	39	19 Jan. 1736	21 Jan. 1736	LESLIE (John) of Findraffie—Lands and eftate of *Findraffie,* and others.	MURRAY and ROSS.
308	9	97	29 July 1736	18 Nov. 1736	LAUCHTANE (Thomas) *alias* M'Laughlan, of Green—Lands and eftate of *Gallowbog,* and others.	DUNBARTON.
310	9	110	4 Jan. 1737	7 Jan. 1737	LOCKHART (Sir James) of Carftairs—Lands of *Collumbie* and *Walls,* and others.	LANERK.
311	9	119	16 Apr. 1733	29 July 1737	LOCKHART (Allan) of Cleghorn—Lands and barony of *Cleghorn,* and others.	LANERK.

No.	Vol.	Fol.	Date of Tailzie.	Date of Regist.	ENTAILERS NAMES and LANDS.	SHIRES.
					L, Continued.	
319	9	248	21 Dec. 1738	20 Jan. 1739	LOTHIAN (William, Marquis of) —Lordfhip and barony of *New-bottle*, and others.	EDINBURGH, ROX-BURGH, and BER-WICK.
323	9	358	26 Oct. 1737	15 Jan. 1740	LAUDER (George) of Pitfcand-ly—Lands and eftate of *Pitf-candly*, and others.	FORFAR.
325	9	372	14 Jan. 1741	16 Jan. 1741	LOVAT (Simon, Lord)—Lands, lordfhip and barony of *Lovat*.	INVERNESS.
345	10	191	27 July 1743	30 July 1743	LOCKHART (Allan) of Cleghorn —Lands and eftate of *Badro-nald*, and others.	LANERK.
385	11	239	3 Jan. 1749	11 Jan. 1749	LOCKHART (Sir James) of Car-ftairs—Lands and barony of *Carftairs*, and others.	LANERK.
400	12	12	1 July 1751	18 July 1751	LOCKHART (Sir James) of Car-ftairs—Obligement by him, difcharging the power of alter-ing his tailzie.	LANERK.
435	12	387	11 Dec. 1755	22 Jan. 1756	LAUDERDALE (James, Earl of) —Lands, barony, and regality of *Thirleftane*, and others.	BERWICK, EDIN-BURGH, and RENFREW.

No.	Vol.	Fol.	Date of Tailzie.	Date of Regift.	ENTAILERS NAMES and LANDS.	SHIRES.
					L, *Continued.*	
436	12	400	19Apr.1753	5 Mar. 1756	LUMSDAIN (John) of Balnearn, writer to the fignet—-Lands and eftate of *Balnearn*, and barony of *Lumfdain.*	FIFE and BERWICK.
492	14	246	7 Oct. 1758	27June1764	LITTLEJOHN (Alexander) of Woodfton—Lands and eftate of *Hall, Woodfton*, and others.	KINCARDINE.
507	14	464	24Dec.1764	19Nov.1766	LE GRAND (Alexander) of Bonnington—Lands and eftate of *Bonnington.*	EDINBURGH.
515	15	18	25Sept.1766	19Dec.1767	LANG (Gabriel) merchant in Greenock—Lands and eftate of *Meikle Overtoun of Colquhoun*, and others.	DUNBARTON.
575	17	85	23Nov.1771	26Nov.1771	LEITH (Alexander) of Freefield—Lands and baronies of *Freefield, Towrie*, and *Glenkindy.*	ABERDEEN and KINCARDINE.
618	18	358	6 Jan. 1775	16Feb.1775	LEITH (Alexander) of Freefield—Contract of marriage betwixt him and Mifs Mary Gordon, containing entail of eftate of *Glenkindy.*	ABERDEEN.

Y

No.	Vol.	Fol.	Date of Tailzie	Date of Regift.	ENTAILERS NAMES and LANDS.	SHIRES.
					L, *Continued.*	
633	19	109	28 Dec. 1775	2 Mar. 1776	LAUDERDALE (James, Earl of)——*Several Lands belonging to him in the shires of*	BERWICK, EDINBURGH, and LINLITHGOW.
639	19	195	20 Oct. 1775	23 Nov. 1776	LOCKHART-DENHAM (Sir William) of Westshields—— Lands and estate of *Westshields.*	LANERK.
——	19	201	23 Apr. 1776	23 Nov. 1776	LOCKHART-DENHAM (Sir William)—Nomination of tutors and curators relative to the above entail.	LANERK.
——	19	203	31 Jan. 1776	23 Nov. 1776	LOCKHARTS (Susanna and Jean)—Ratification by them of said entail of *Westshields.*	LANERK.
——	19	207	14 Aug. 1776	23 Nov. 1776	LOCKHART (Mrs. Susanna)—Tailzie by her of said lands of *Westshields.*	LANERK.
650	19	364	5 July 1777	30 July 1777	LOCKHART, *alias* PORTERFIELD (Mary) widow of John Lockhart of Lee——Certain parts of the lands and estate of *Lee* and *Cartland.*	LANERK.

No.	Vo!	Fol.	Date of Tailzie	Date of Regist	ENTAILERS NAMES and LANDS.	SHIRES.
					L, *Continued.*	
568	20	155	10July 1764	3 Mar. 1775	LOTHIAN (William, Marquis of) therein defigned Earl of Ancram—Lands of *Eaftmains*, and *Eaftwood of Dalhoufie*, called *Haukhill*.	EDINBURGH.
686	20	302	24 May 1780	10 Aug. 1780	LAMONT (Alexander) of Knockdow—-Lands of *Inverchellan* and *Lochnagatt*, and others.	ARGYLE.

.

No.	Vol.	Fol.	Date of Tailzie.	Date of Regift.	ENTAILERS NAMES and LANDS.	SHIRES.
					M.	
4	1	27	4 June 1689	19 July 1692	M'KENZIE (Sir George) of Rofe-haugh—-Lands and eftate of *Rofehaugh.*	FORFAR.
6	1	44	3 Dec. 1688	8 Feb. 1694	M'KENZIE (Roderick) of Pre-ftonhall—Lands and eftate of *Preftonhall.*	EDINBURGH.
11	1	96	4 Dec. 1688	4 July 1694	M'KENZIE (George, Vifcount of Tarbet)—-Eftates of *Tarbet,* *Cromarty,* and *Royfton.*	ROSS, &c.
38	2	167	3 April 1696	29 Feb. 1700	M'KIE (John) of Larg—-Lands and eftate of *Larg.*	KIRKCUDBRIGHT.
39	2	180	27 May 1698	14 June 1700	MORAY (Alexander, Earl of)—Lordfhip of *Abernethic,* and o-thers.	ELGIN & FORRES, INVERNESS, PERTH, and FIFE.
42	2	219	20 Jan. 1700	30 July 1700	MAITLAND (Sir Charles) of Pit-richie—Lands of *Pitrichie,* and others.	ABERDEEN.
48	2	326	29 Jan. 1701	20 Feb. 1701	M'KENZIE (John) fon of Sir A-lexander M'Kenzie of Coull—Lands and eftate of *Eafter* and *Wefter Comries.*	ROSS.

z

No.	Vol.	Fol.	Date of Tailzie.	Date of Regn.	ENTAILERS NAMES and LANDS.	SHIRES.
					M, *Continued.*	
49	2	,62	27 Aug 1700	28 Feb. 1701	MENZIES (Gilbert) of Pitfod-dels—Eftate of *Pitfoddels,* and others.	ABERDEEN and KINCARDINE.
58	3	90	9 Jan. 1701	10 July 1703	MAXWELL (Sir William) of Calderwood—Lands and eftate of *Calderwood,* and others.	LANERK.
60	3	101	3 Mar. 1703	28 July 1703	MAXWELL (Sir William) of Monreith—Lands and eftate of *Monreith,* and others.	WIGTOUN.
64	3	137	25 Dec. 1691	14 Feb. 1704	MENZIES (James) of Schien—Lands and eftate of *Schien.*	PERTH.
69	3	189	6 April 1704	12 July 1704	MONTGOMERY (Sir Robert) of Skelmorly—Lands and eftate of *Skelmorly,* and others.	AYR & RENFREW.
82	3	347	9 Feb. 1706	18 Feb. 1706	M'KENZIE (Roderick) of Pre-ftonhall, one of the Lords of Seffion—Lands and eftate of *Preftonhall.*	INVERNESS.
91	4	11	5 Dec. 1703	25 Mar. 1707	M'GILL (Robert) of Fingafk—Lands and barony of *Fingafk,* and others.	PERTH.

No.	Vol.	Fol.	Date of Tailzie	Date of Regift.	ENTAILERS NAMES and LANDS.	SHIRES.
					M, *Continued.*	
110	4	197	9 Aug 1707	21 July 1710	M'GREGOR (Evan) of New-haven—Lands in *Newbaven.*	EDINBURGH.
113	4	227	12 Dec. 1710	28 Feb. 1711	MURRAY. (Robert) of Pulroffie—Lands and eftate of *Pulroffie,* and others.	SUTHERLAND.
114	4	234	17 Oct. 1710	9 June 1711	MORAY (Charles, Earl of)—Lands, lordfhip, and earldom of *Moray.*	ELGIN and FORRES, FIFE, EDIN-BURGH, and IN-VERNESS.
117	4	268	18 May 1710	19 July 1711	MAXWELLS (Janet and Agnes) of Breadiland—Lands and e-ftate of *Breadiland.*	RENFREW.
135	5	60	16 July 1714	19 Nov. 1714	MORAY (Charles, Earl of)—Lands and barony of *Camilla.*	PERTH.
141	5	112	31 July 1689	6 July 1716	MERCER (Sir James) of Aldie—Lands and barony of *Meikle-our.*	PERTH.
142	5	117	27 June 1715	6 July 1716	MERCER (Sir Laurence) of Al-die—Lands and barony of *Meikleour,* and others.	PERTH & KINROSS.

No.	Vol.	Fol.	Date of Tailzie.	Date of Regist.	ENTAILERS NAMES and LANDS.	SHIRES.
					M, *Continued.*	
150	5	187	14 Apr. 1716	17 Dec. 1718	M'LELLAN (Robert) of Barclay—Lands and eftate of *Barclay*, and others.	KIRKCUDBRIGHT.
162	5	284	16 Aug. 1720	1 Dec. 1720	MERCER (Mrs. Jean) of Aldie—Lands and barony of *Meikleour*, and others.	PERTH & KINROSS.
163	5	300	6 Aug. 1720	2 Dec. 1720	MYRETOUN (Sir Andrew) of Gogar—Lands and barony of *Gogar*, and others.	EDINBURGH.
170	5	367	9 June 1722	30 June 1722	MAXWELL (John) of Middlebie—Lands and eftate of *Middlebie*, and others.	DUMFRIES.
172	5	382	6 June 1722	18 July 1722	MURRAY (Sir Patrick) of Ochtertyre—Lands and baronies of *Ochtertyre*, *Foulis*, and *Monivaird*.	PERTH.
173	5	392	14 May 1722	25 July 1722	MERCER (Sir Laurence) of Aldie—Lands and barony of *Lethindy*, and others.	PERTH.
174	5	113	14 May 1722	25 July 1722	MERCER (faid Sir Laurence)—Lands and eftate of *Littlebair*, and others.	PERTH.

No.	Vol.	Fol.	Date of Tailzie.	Date of Regift.	ENTAILERS NAMES and LANDS.	SHIRES.
					M, *Continued.*	
177	6	35	25Feb. 1709	5 Dec. 1722	M'KAY (George) of Bighoufes—Lands and eftate of *Bighoufes,* and others.	SUTHERLAND.
184	6	90	17Nov.1703	13Nov.1723	M'KENZIE (Kenneth) of Dundonnel—Lands and eftate of *Auchtadonnel,* and others.	ROSS.
188	6	132	13Sept.1710	1 Feb. 1724	MURRAY (Sir Alexander) of Melgund—Lands and barony of *Melgund,* and others.	FORFAR.
195	6	233	24Sept.1724	12Nov.1724	MALCOM (Margaret) daughter of John Malcom of Balbeddie—Lands and eftate of *Grange,* and others.	FIFE.
207	6	307	13Sept.1710	23Dec.1725	MURRAY (Sir Alexander) of Melgund—Lands and eftate of *Melgund* and *Kinninmond.*	FORFAR.
210	6	331	21Feb. 1726	25Feb. 1726	MURRAY (Sir Patrick) of Ochtertyre—Lands and barony of *Ochtertyre,* and others.	PERTH.

No.	Vol.	Fol.	Date of Tailzie	Date of Regist.	ENTAILERS NAMES and LANDS.	SHIRES.
					M, *Continued.*	
211	6	345	24 Sept 1723	25 Feb. 1726	MURRAY (Sir Alexander) of Blackbarrony—Lands and baronies of *Hatton-Murray*, alias *Blackbarrony*, and others.	PEEBLES.
214	6	362	22 June 1726	14 July 1726	MORAY (Earl of)—Tailzie of *The Heritable Office of Sheriff of the Shires of Elgin and Forres* —And	ELGIN & FORRES.
					Procuratory for refigning the fortification called the Citadel of *Invernefs.*	INVERNESS.
216	6	381	30 May 1697	29 July 1726	MENZIES (Colonel James) of Culdares—Lands and eftate of *Culdares* and *Tynáffie*, and others.	PERTH.
245	7	281	29 May 1727	7 Nov. 1729	MURRAY (Patrick) of Pitlochrie—Lands and eftate of *Pitlochrie.*	FIFE.
252	7	357	22 June 1727	17 July 1730	M'DOWAL (James) of Gillefpie—Tailzie of lands of *Gillefpie* and *Craignarget*, and nomination by him in favour of Alexander M'Dowal of Garthland.	WIGTOUN.

No.	Vol.	Fol.	Date of Tailzie.	Date of Regift.	ENTAILERS NAMES and LANDS.	SHIRES.
					M, *Continued.*	
256	8	1	16 July 1730	7 Nov. 1730	MONCRIEFF (Sir Thomas)—— Lands and barony of *Moncrieff*, and others.	PERTH.
257	8	11	19 Nov. 1730	8 Dec. 1730	MORAY (Charles, Earl of)—— Lordfhip and earldom of *Moray*, and others.	INVERNESS, EL-GIN & FORRES, FIFE, PERTH, EDINBURGH, and LINLITHGOW.
258	8	56	19 Nov. 1730	8 Dec. 1730	MORAY (Charles, Earl of)—— The barony of *Camilla*.	FIFE.
261	8	87	21 July 1730	24 Feb. 1731	MORRISON (William) younger of Preftongrange—Lands and eftate of *Craigleith*.	MID-LOTHIAN.
263	8	110	31 May 1720	27 Feb. 1731	MAXWELL (John) of Dargavel —Tailzie, and nomination relative thereto, of lands of *Dargavel*, and others.	RENFREW.
268	8	181	1 June 1732	14 June 1732	MURRAY (William) of Touchadam and Polmaife—Lands and barony of *Cowie*, and others.	STIRLING.
273	8	245	5 Jan. 1730	10 Jan. 1733	MALCOM (Margaret) of Grange —Lands and eftate of *Grange*.	FIFE.

No.	Vol.	Fol.	Date of Tailzie	Date of Regift.	ENTAILERS NAMES and LANDS.	SHIRES.
					M, *Continued.*	
276	8	266	9 Oct. 1725	5 July 1733	MALCOM (Michael) of Balbeddie—Lands and barony of *Nuthill*, and others.	PERTH & FIFE.
287	8	358	1 Jan. 1734	29 Jan. 1734	MURRAY (William) of Touchadam and Polmaife—Eik, tailzie, and additional claufes and provifions to his tailzie, N° 268.	STIRLING.
294	8	419	27 May 1728	25 Feb. 1735	MONTGOMERY (Sir Hugh) of Skelmorlie—Lands and eftate of *Lochlibofide*, and *Hartfield*, and others.	RENFREW & AYR.
298	9	7	20 Mar. 1735	27 June 1735	MURRAY (William) of Touchadam—Tailzie in his favours by John Nairn of Greenyards—Lands of *Ingramfcruife*.	STIRLING.
299	9	20	28 Feb. and 3 Mar. 1735	15 July 1735	MORAY (Charles, Earl of) James Stewart, and others, in favours of the Countefs of Aboyne—Lands of *Pittendreich*, and others.	ELGIN & FORRES.
303	9	45	1 June 1736	10 June 1736	MORTON (John) merchant in Kilmarnock—Lands of *Boreland*, and others.	AYR.

No.	Vol.	Fol.	Date of Tailzie.	Date of Regift.	ENTAILERS NAMES and LANDS.	SHIRE.
					M, *Continued.*	
335	10	92	16 Apr. 1741	15 Jan. 1742	MURRAY (Sir Alexander) of Blackbarrony—Lands and barony of *Hatton-Murray*, alias *Blackbarrony*.	PEEBLES.
337	10	111	9 Oct. 1742	6 Nov. 1742	M'DOUGAL (John) of Arncaple—Lands and estate of *Arncaple*, and others.	ARGYLE.
341	10	156	19 Jan. 1709	14 June 1743	MAXWELL (James) of Merkfworth, merchant in Glafgow—Lands and estate of *Merkfworth*, and others.	RENFREW.
342	10	169	16 Apr. 1745	17 June 1743	M'KENZIE (Sir George) of Grandville, and Sir James M'Kenzie of Royfton—Mutual tailzie by them of lands of *Coulkenzie*, *Craigmill*, and others.	ROSS&CROMARTY
349	10	229	25 Apr. 1739	2 Feb. 1744	MURRAY (Robert) of Murrayfhall—Tailzie by him to Robert Keith of Craig, of lands of *Murrayfhall*, and others.	PEEBLES.

No.	Vol.	Fol.	Date of Tailzie.	Date of Regift.	ENTAILERS NAMES and LANDS.	SHIRES.
					· M, *Continued.*	
359	10	362	10 & 29 June & July 1690.	11 July 1745	M'CULLOCH (James) of Piltoun—Tailzie in his favour by James Barbour, of lands of *Muldarg*.	ROSS.
360	10	378	12 Aug. 1742	23 July 1745	M'CRAE (James) of Orangefield—Tailzie by him in favour of Elizabeth M'Quire, Countefs of Glencairn, of the barony of *Ochiltree*.	AYR.
361	10	389	12 Aug. 1742	23 July 1745	M'CRAE (faid James)—Tailzie by him in favour of James M'Quire, of the barony of *Houftoun*.	RENFREW.
362	10	399	12 Aug. 1742	23 July 1745	M'CRAE (faid James)—Tailzie by him in favour of Mifs M'Crae-M'Quire, of the barony of *Orangefield*, formerly *Monktoun*.	AYR.
375	11	97	22 Apr. 1747	17 July 1747	M'CULLOCH (John) of Barholm, and Jean Gordon his fpoufe—Lands and eftate of *Barholm*, and others.	KIRKCUDBRIGHT.

No.	Vol.	Fol.	Date of Tailzie.	Date of Regift.	ENTAILERS NAMES and LANDS.	SHIRES.
					M, *Continued.*	
376	11	110	30 Mar. 1742	17 July 1747	M'CULLOCH (faid John) and fpoufe—-Lands and eftate of *Culvennan*, and others.	WIGTOUN.
408	12	74	27 Oct. 1752	3 Mar. 1753	M'KENZIE (Sir Alexander) of Garloch—-Lands and barony of *Garloch*, and others.	ROSS.
410	12	96	16 Nov. 1751	9 Mar. 1753	MOODIE (Roger) collector of the fhore-dues at Leith—-*Certain Houfes and Lands in and about Edinburgh, and fonre Acres of Land in the barony of Brough-ton.*	EDINBURGH.
426	12	286	18 May 1754	11 Mar. 1755	M'LEAN (Hector) of Coll—— Tailzie, and additional deed relative thereto, of lands and barony of *Coll*, and others.	ARGYLE.
437	12	111	17 Mar. 1753	4 Aug. 1756	MILLER (William) of Glenlee —Lands and barony of *Glen-lee*, and others.	KIRKCUDBRIGHT.
440	12	433	10 Jan. 1756	3 Mar. 1757	MURRAY (William) of Touch-adam—Lands and barony of *Touchadam*, and others, and rental of faid lands, relative thereto.	STIRLING.

No.	Vol.	Fol.	Date of Tailzie.	Date of Regift.	ENTAILERS NAMES and LANDS.	SHIRES.
					M, *Continued.*	
443	13	24	30 Dec. 1754	15 June 1757	MUIR (Robert) of Glenquicken—Lands and barony of *Living-stone*, and others.	KIRKCUDBRIGHT.
448	13	74	1, 2, & 4 Nov. 1757	4 Jan. 1758	MONTGOMERY (Alexander) of Coilsfield—Lands and estate of *Outmains of Coilsfield*, and others.	AYR.
450	13	109	23 Nov. 1752	17 Feb. 1758	M'CULLOCH (Edward) of Ard-wall—Lands and estate of *Ard-wall, Irelandtoun*, and others.	KIRKCUDBRIGHT.
454	13	167	23 June 1758	10 Aug. 1758	M'DOUGALL (John) of Ardin-caple—Lands and estate of *Ardincaple*, and others.	ARGYLE.
456	13	184	3 April 1756	24 Jan. 1759	M'DOUAL (Andrew) of Bank-ton, one of the Senators of the College of Justice—Lands of *Corrochtree*, and others.	WIGTOUN, HAD-DINGTON, and PEEBLES.
480	14	68	29 Dec. 1762	13 Jan. 1763	M'CULLOCH (John) of Bar-holm—Lands and estate of *Barholm*, and others.	KIRKCUDBRIGHT.
489	14	167	14 Apr. 1761	26 Jan. 1764	MUNRO (Mrs. Mary) of New-more—Lands and estate of *Newmore*, and others.	ROSS & SUTHER-LAND.

No.	Vol.	Fol.	Date of Regist.	Date of Tailzie.	ENTAILERS NAMES and LANDS.	SHIRES.
					M, *Continued.*	
499	14	343	27 Apr. 1764	21 June 1765	M'GILL, *alias* KELSO (Mrs. Mary) and Jean Kelfo her fifter—Lands of *Dankeith*, and others.	AYR.
502	14	406	26 July 1765	10 Aug. 1765	M'DOUGALL (Alexander) of Dunnollie—Lands of *Dunolichbeg*, and others.	ARGYLE.
513	14	526	16 July 1763	8 Aug. 1767	M'LAUCHLAN (John) of Kilchoan—-Lands and eftate of *Kilchoan*, and others.	ARGYLE.
519	15	75	12 Jan. 1762	22 Jan. 1768	MUNRO (David) of Allan, writer to the fignet—-Lands of *Meikle Allan*, and others.	ROSS.
530	15	378	15 July 1768	30 July 1768	MERCER (William) of Aldie—Lands and eftate of *Kincleven*.	PERTH.
533	15	417	11 Aug. 1759	15 Nov. 1768	MEAN (William) of Barneight—-Lands and eftate of *Barneight*, and others.	WICTOUN.
534	15	424	16 Oct. 1767	23 Nov. 1768	MORTON (James, Earl of)—-Lands and barony of *Dalmahoy*, and others.	EDINBURGH.

C c

No.	Vol.	Fol.	Date of Tailzie	Date of Regift.	ENTAILERS NAMES and LANDS.	SHIRES.
					M, Continued.	
535	15	424	16 Oct. 1767	23 Nov. 1768	MORTON (faid James, Earl of) —Lordfhip of *Aberdour*, and others.	EDINBURGH.
539	16	34	14 Mar. 1769	22 June 1769	MORAY (James) of Abercairny —Lands and barony of *Abercairny*, and others.	PERTH.
557	16	335	5 Apr. 1763	8 Mar. 1771	M'DONALD (John) of Largie— Lands and eftate of *Largie*, and others.	ARGYLE.
567	16	491	28 May 1763	3 July 1771	MURRAY (John) of Blackbarrony, *alias* Stewart, of Afcog ——Lands of *Afcog*, and others.	BUTE & ARGYLE.
573	17	51	1 Dec. 1767	9 Aug. 1771	M'NEIL (John) of Firefergus— Lands and eftate of *Firefergus*, *Largybane*, and others.	ARGYLE.
581	17	193	11 Mar. 1754	26 June 1772	M'KENZIE-STEWART (James) of Rofchaugh, Lord Privy Seal —Tailzie of certain parts of *Markmyre*, and others.	PERTH & FORFAR.

No.	Vol.	Fol.	Date of Tailzie.	Date of Regift.	ENTAILERS NAMES and LANDS.	SHIRES.
					M, *Continued.*	
582	17	193	12 Aug. 1758	26 June 1772	Another entail by said James M'Kenzie-Stewart, of a third part of a fourth part of the town and lands of *Balmaw.*	FORFAR.
582	17	—	7 July 1764	26 June 1772	Another entail by him, of the half of the lands of *Easter Keilour,* and others.	FORFAR.
584	17	—	14 Jan. 1772	26 June 1772	Another entail by him, of the lands and estate of *Belmont*—All the above four entails lying contiguous to the estates of Newtyle and Achtertyre.	PERTH.
625	18	476	10 Apr. 1770	27 June 1775	M'FARLANE-BROWN (William) of Kirktoun—Lands and estate of *Ballancleroch.*	STIRLNG.
628	19	1	9 Aug. 1775	9 Dec. 1775	MENZIES (James and Archibald) elder and younger of Culdares—Tailzie by them of the lands of *Stix,* and others, in favour of John, Earl of Breadalbane.	PERTH.

No.	Vol.	Fol.	Date of Tailzie.	Date of Regift.	ENTAILERS NAMES and LANDS.	SHIRES.
					M, *Continued.*	
629	19	36	9 Aug. 1775	9 Dec. 1775	MENZIES (James) of Culdares—Entail in his favour by John, Earl of Breadalbane, of the lands of *Kenknock*, and others.	PERTH.
640	19	218	28 Nov. 1776	23 Nov. 1776	MURRAY (John) of Philiphaugh—Lands and eftate of *Philiphaugh.*	SELKIRK.
643	19	285	9 Aug. 1756	5 Feb. 1777	MONTGOMERY (Mrs. Anne) of Kirktonholm—Lands and barony of *Kirktonholm*, and others.	LANERK and AYR.
644	19	301	1 Sept. 1761	5 Feb. 1777	MONTGOMERY - CUNNINGHAM (Captain Alexander)—Lands and eftate of *Corfehill*, and others.	LANERK and AYR.
648	19	351	27 May 1774	30 July 1777	MORAY (James) of Abercairny—Lands and eftate of *Abernyte*—And	PERTH.
649	19	—	30 July 1774	30 July 1777	Another entail by him of the lands of *Miltoun of Abernyte.*	PERTH.

No.	Vol.	Fol.	Date of Tailzie	Date of Regist.	ENTAILERS NAMES and LANDS.	SHIRES.
					M, *Continued.*	
660	19	522	28 Apr. 1775	13 Jan. 1779	M'DOUGAL (Dame Barbara) with confent of Sir George Hay-M'Dougal her hufband, —The lands and barony of *Mackerflon*, and others.	ROXBURGH.
663	20	44	18 Nov. 1778	11 Feb. 1779	MENZIES (Sir Robert) of that Ilk—-Lands of *Menzies, Rannoch*, and others.	PERTH.
664	20	63	26 Mar. 1701	16 Feb. 1779	MENZIES (James) of Culdares— Contract of feu betwixt the Duke of Athole and the tutors of faid James Menzies, containing tailzie of lands and barony of *Glenlyon*.	PERTH.
665	20	86	18 and 29 May 1703.	16 Feb. 1779	Another contract of feu betwixt faid parties, narrating the above, and containing tailzie of faid lands and barony of *Glenlyon*.	PERTH.
666	20	103	30 Apr. 1773	16 Feb. 1779	MENZIES (James and Archibald) of Culdares—Tailzie of the lands and barony of *Culdares* and *Glenlyon*, and others.	PERTH & FORFAR.

D d

No.	Vol.	Fol.	Date of Tailzie.	Date of Regist	ENTAILERS NAMES and LANDS.	SHIRES.
					M, *Continued.*	
667	20	125	7 Oct. 1776	16 Feb. 1779	MENZIES (Archibald) of Cúldares——Tailzie of lands and eftate of *Kenknock*, and others.	PERTH.
669	20	163	14 Apr. 1777	22 July 1779	M'DOUAL (John) of Logan and Bankton—Lands and eftate of *Logan.*	WIGTOUN.
672	20	210	28 and 30 July 1694.	11 Dec. 1779	M'KENZIE (George) fon of Sir George M'Kenzie of Rofehaugh——Tailzie in his favour by James Ramfay younger of Banff, of lands of *Bandochie* and *Coupar Maccoultrie.*	PERTH.
673	20	222	23 Aug. 1775	11 Dec. 1779	M'DOUGAL (Alexander) of Sorroba—Lands and eftate of *Sorroba,* and others.	ARGYLE.
679	20	304	25 Jan. 1778	10 Mar. 1780	M'DOUALL (John) of Logan—Lands and eftate of *Culgrotte.*	WIGTOUN.

No.	Vol	Fol.	Date of Tailzie.	Date of Regiſt.	ENTAILERS NAMES and LANDS.	Shire.
					M, *Continued.*	
704	21	204	28 June 1776	7 Dec. 1781	MUNRO (Sir Hary) of Foulis—Lands, barony and eſtate of *Foulis,* and others.	RUSS.
720	21	505	31 Jan. 1783	5 Mar. 1783	MURRAY (Sir William) of Ochtertyre—Lands of *Calandermore* and *Calanderbeg.*	PERTH.

No.	Vol.	Fol.	Date of Tailzie.	Date of Regift.	ENTAILERS NAMES *and* LANDS.	Sbires.
					N.	
16	1	177	29Sept.1687	13Dec.1695	NISBET (Sir John) of Dirleton—Lands and eftate of *Dirleton*.	CLACKMANNAN.
103	4	149	19Nov.1709	12Jan.1710	NAESMITH (Sir James) of Poffo—Lands and barony of *Poffo*, and others.	PEEBLES.
118	4	277	18Sept.1691	8 Nov.1711	NAIRN (Lord and Lady)—Lands of *Strathurd*, and others.	PERTH.
169	5	359	6Sept.1711	14June1722	NICOLSON (Dame Helenor) relict of Sir John Shaw of Greenock—Lands of *Carnock, Plam*, and others.	STIRLING.
202	6	287	5 Sept.1722	12June1725	NISBET (William) of Dirleton—Lands of *Reftalrig*.	EDINBURGH.
206	6	301	18June1724	14Dec.1725	NEWTON (Sir Richard) of Newton—Lands and barony of *Newton*.	EDINBURGH.
212	6	35c	12Nov.1723	21June1726	NORVAL (George) of Boghall—Lands and barony of *Boghall*, and others.	LINLITHGOW.
280	8	308	8 June 1733	28July 1733	NEILSON (Robert) of Barncailzie—Lands and eftate of *Barncailzie*, and others.	KIRKCUDBRIGHT.

E e

No.	Vol.	Fol.	Date of Tailzie.	Date of Regist.	ENTAILERS NAMES and LANDS.	SHIRES.
					N, *Continued.*	
296	8	134	22May 1730	12June1735	NAIRN (Mrs. Barbara)—Lands and barony of *Seggieden.*	PERTH.
298	9	7	20Mar.1735	27June1735	NAIRN (John) of Greenyeards —Tailzie in favour of William Murray of Touchadam, of lands of *Ingramfcruife,* and others.	STIRLING.
307	9	83	14Feb. 1705	10July 1736	NAIRN (Agnes) relict of the deceafed William Blair of Tarfappie—Lands of *Drumkilbo,* and others, entailed in her favour by John, Lord Balmarino.	PERTH.
340	10	147	27Apr. 1742	8 June 1743	NICOLSON (Sir William) of Glenbervie—Lands and barony of *Glenbervie,* and others.	KINCARDINE.
384	11	219	22Nov.1748	3 Jan. 1749	NAPIER (James) of Ballakinrain —Lands of *Ballakinrain,* and others.	
					Revocation of this tailzie is dated 17th October 1754, and recorded in the books of Seffion, 4th December 1754, (office Meffrs. Juftice and Kirkpatrick.)	STIRLING.

No.	Vol.	Fol.	Date of Tailzie.	Date of Regift.	ENTAILERS NAMES and LANDS.	SHIRES.
					N, *Continued.*	
465	13	280	9 July 1760	15 July 1760	NICOLSON (Sir William) of Glenbervie——Nomination of heirs by him.	KINCARDINE.
496	14	308	7 Oct. 1763	4 Dec. 1764	NICOLSON (Lady Dame) Elizabeth Carnegie, relict of Sir James Nicolson—*All Lands and Heritable Subjects that should belong to her at her death.*	EDINBURGH.
596	18	1	20 May 1719	30 June 1773	NAPIER (Francis, Lord)—Lands of *Bouirhope, Thirleftane,* and others, entailed by Sir William Scott of Thirleftane his father.	SELKIRK.

No.	Vol.	Fol.	Date of Tailzie.	Date of Regift.	ENTAILERS NAMES and LANDS.	SHIRES.
					O.	
33	2	108	30Sept.1697	18Nov.1698	OSWALD (Thomas) of Fingalton—Lands and eftate of *Fingalton*.	EDINBURGH.
79	3	302	28Mar.1705	29Dec.1705	OXFORD (Robert, Vifcount of)—Lands and barony of *Cranfton-M'Gill*, and others.	EDINBURGH.
248	7	304	23Dec.1729	6 Feb. 1730	OGILVIE (David) of Clunie—Lands and eftate of *Mains of Craigie*, and others.	PERTH & FORFAR.
255	7	401	29Dec.1729	29July 1730	OLIPHANT (Patrick) of Bachilton—Town and lands of *Bachilton*, and others.	PERTH.
367	11	16	24Aug.1719	25June1746	OLIPHANT (James) of Gafk—Lands and barony of *Gafk*.	PERTH.
479	14	54	13Sept.1762	27Nov.1762	OGILVIE (James) of Baldevie—Lands of *Baldevie*, lately called *Eafter* and *Wefter Boynfield*, and lands of *Bagall*.	BANFF.

F f

No.	Vol.	Fol.	Date of Tailzie.	Date of Regift.	ENTAILERS NAMES *and* LANDS.	S H I R E S.
					P.	
167	5	336	19 & 21 Oct. 1721.	12 Dec. 1721	PORTERFIELD (Alexander) of that Ilk—Lands and eſtate of *Auchinſoyle,* and others.	RENFREW & AYR.
247	7	299	10 Jan. 1730	14 Jan. 1730	PARK (Alexander) maltman in Paiſley—*Some Houſes and Acres in the town and territory of Paiſley.*	RENFREW.
386	11	244	3 Feb. 1742	26 Jan. 1749	PRESTON (Major General George)——Lands and barony of *Valeyfield, Innerkeithing,* and others—With power and faculty relative thereto.	PERTH, FIFE, STIRLING, and EDINBURGH.
395	11	419	3 Nov. 1750	7 Nov. 1750	POLLOCK (Sir Robert) of that Ilk—Lands and barony of *Over Pollock,* and others.	RENFREW.
402	12	19	29 Jan. 1743	19 Dec. 1751	PATERSON (Sir John) of Eccles—Lands and barony of *Eccles,* and others.	BERWICK.

No.	Vol.	Fol.	Date of Tailzie.	Date of Regift.	ENTAILERS/NAMES and LANDS.	SHIRES.
					P, *Continued.*	
434	12	383	22 Oct. 1755	15 Nov. 1755	PATERSON (faid Sir John) of Eccles—Deed of alteration of his tailzie.	BERWICK.
549	16	193	6 June 1770	26 June 1770	POLLOCK (Sir Robert) of that Ilk—Lands and barony of *Pollock.*	RENFREW.
556	16	297	Difpofition dated 13 Aug 1759. Decreet dated 11 Aug. 1770.	21 Dec. 1770	PRINGLE (George) of Newhall—Decreet of proving the tenor of a difpofition and tailzie by him of his lands of *Newhall,* and others.	FIFE.
615	18	315	23 Dec. 1774	25 Jan. 1775	POLLOCK (Sir Robert) of that Ilk—Lands and barony of O-ver *Pollock,* and others.	RENFREW.
650	19	364	5 July 1777	30 July 1777	PORTERFIELD, *alias* LOCK-HART (Mary) widow of John Lockhart of Lee—Parts of the lands and eftate of *Lee* and *Cartland.*	LANERK.
677	20	282	10 Aug. 1776	7 Mar. 1780	PRIMROSE (Edward) of Burn-brae—Lands and eftate of *Burnbrae,* and others.	PERTH.

No.	Vol.	Fol.	Date of Tailzie.	Date of Regist.	ENTAILERS NAMES and LANDS.	SHIRES.
					P, Continued.	
678	20	293	23 Apr. 1673	9 Mar. 1780	PRIMROSE (Sir Archibald) of Cairnton—Lands of *Dumenay*, alias *Dalmeny*, and others, in favour of the Earl of Rofeberry.	LINLITHGOW.
706	21	226	12 Oct. 1781	22 Jan. 1782	PANMURE (William, Earl of) ——Lands and baronies of *Panmure, Aberbrothock, Brechin, Navar, Edzell, Lethnet, Lochlie, Kellie, Ballumbie*, and others.	FORFAR.

No.	Vol.	Fol.	Date of Tailzie.	Date of Regist.	ENTAILERS NAMES and LANDS.	SHIRES.

Q.

No.	Vol.	Fol.	Date of Tailzie.	Date of Regist.	ENTAILERS NAMES and LANDS.	SHIRES.
185	6	142	26 Dec. 1705	21 Feb. 1724	QUEENSBERRY AND DOVER (Duke of)——Lands and baronies of *Drumlanrig*, and others.	DUMFRIES.
546	16	138	17 July 1769	9 Feb. 1770	QUEENSBERRY AND DOVER (Duke of)—-Certain lands in the county of Dumfries, lying contiguous to the entailed estate of *Queensberry*.	DUMFRIES.
699	11	129	12 Oct. 1693	11 Aug. 1781	QUEENSBERRY (William, Duke of) and his son Lord William Douglas——Contract of marriage betwixt said Lord William and Lady Jean Hay, second daughter of John, Earl of Tweeddale, containing tailzie of the lordship of *Neidpath*, and others.	PEEBLES.

No.	Vol.	Fol.	Date of Regift.	Date of Tailzie	ENTAILERS NAMES and LANDS.	SHIRES.
					R.	
2	1	6	22 May 1685	26 Feb. 1691	ROSS (David) of Balnagowan—Lands and eſtate of *Balnagowan.*	ROSS,
21	2	1	3 Sept. 1691	9 June 1696	ROCHEAD (James) of Inverleith—Lands and eſtate of *Inverleith,* and others.	EDINBURGH and BERWICK.
62	3	121	7 Dec. 1703	20 Jan. 1704	ROBERTSON (William) of Inches, and John Robertſon his ſon—Lands of *Eaſter Leys, Leyſcrune, Meiklehilltoun,* and others.	INVERNESS.
88	3	411	11 Oct. 1706	8 Mar. 1707	ROSS (David) of Balnagowan, and Francis Stewart of Frankfield—Lands and barony of *Balnagowan,* and others.	ROSS and SUTHERLAND.
96	4	81	3 Sept. 1707	20 Dec. 1707	ROSS (William, Lord) and David Roſs of Balnagowan—Lands and barony of *Balnagowan,* and others.	ROSS.
13	5	72	19 Sept. 1713	15 Jan. 1715	ROSS (John) of Innernothie—Lands and barony of *Hillcairny.*	PERTH.

No.	Vol.	Fol.	Date of Tailzie.	Date of Regist.	ENTAILERS NAMES and LANDS.	SHIRES.
					R, Continued.	
152	5	199	19 Nov. 1681	20 Feb. 1719	RUTHERFOORD (Andrew) of Edgertoun—Lands and barony of Edgertoun.	SELKIRK.
166	5	329	26 Oct. 1674	4 Nov. 1721	RUTHVEN (David, Lord) of Freeland—Lands of Kirktoun of Malon, and others.	PERTH.
168	5	353	23 May 1722	7 June 1722	ROSS (William) of Aldie—Lands and estate of Aldie, and others.	ROSS.
220	7	1	15 Mar. 1725	12 Jan. 1727	ROCHEAD (Dame Janet) relict of Sir David Dalrymple of Hailes—Lands and barony of Melgund, called Northanelgune.	FORFAR.
222	7	39	24 Nov. 1721	14 Feb. 1727	RAMSAY (Sir Andrew) of Whitehill—Lands and estate of Whitehill, and others.	EDINBURGH.
271	8	203	5 Aug. 1727	10 Nov. 1732	ROSS (General Charles) of Balnagowan—Lands and barony of Balnagowan, and others.	ROSS and SUTHERLAND.
301	9	33	15 Jan. 1731	14 Nov. 1735	ROGERS (Andrew) of Daldilling—Lands and estate of Daldilling, and others.	AYR.

No.	Vol.	Fol.	Date of Tailzie	Date of Regist.	ENTAILERS. NAMES and LANDS.	SHIRES.
					R, *Continued.*	
332	10	35	17 May 1706	22 Dec. 1741	RICKART (David) of Riccartoun—Tailzie in his favour by Sir Thomas Burnet of Leys, &c. of lands of *Couton*, and others.	KINCARDINE and ABERDEEN.
365	11	1	30 July 1743	6 June 1746	ROBERTSON (James) writer to the signet—Tailzie in his favour, of the lands and estate of *Cavil*, and others.	FIFE.
417	12	177	14 Jan. 1749	21 Dec. 1753	ROCHEAD (Mrs. Elizabeth) daughter of the deceased Sir James Rochead of Inverleith—The just and equal half of the lands and barony of *Inverleith*—And her just and equal half of the lands of *Darnchester*.	EDINBURGH and BERWICK.
419	12	209	23 Oct. 1751	26 Feb. 1754	ROCHEAD (Colonel James) of Inverleith—Lands of *Carbieston*, and others—And fourth part of the lands of *Inverleith*, and lands of *Darnchester*.	EDINBURGH and BERWICK.
422	12	257	12 Oct. 1706	3 Dec. 1754	ROSS (David) of Balnagowan—Letter of substitution by him, relative to his tailzie, N° 88.	ROSS.

No.	Vol.	Fol.	Date of Tailzie.	Date of Regist.	ENTAILERS NAMES and LANDS.	SHIRES.
					R, *Continued:*	
427	12	294	20June1754	24June1755	REID (Thomas) of Auchinleck—*Mains of Auchinleck, mansion-house, and pertinents.*	FORFAR.
478	14	45	27Jan. 1759	26Nov.1762	RAE (John) of Little Govan—Lands and estate of *Little Go-van,* and others.	LANERK.
503	14	419	7 Oct. 1765	17Dec.1765	RAMSAY-IRVINE (Alexander) of Balmain—Lands and estate of *Newthornton,* and others.	KINCARDINE.
504	14	431	11Mar.1765	18Jan. 1766	ROLLO (Andrew, Lord)—Lands and barony of *Duncrub,* and o-thers.	PERTH & FORFAR.
517	15	38	15May1766	21Jan. 1768	ROSS (Hugh) of Kerse, mer-chant in London—Lands and estate of *Kerse,* and others.	AYR.
520	15	88	Contract dated 23d Aug. 1732. Decreet dated 28th Nov. 1767.	4 Feb. 1768	RAE (Donald, Lord)—Decreet of proving the tenor of a contract of marriage betwixt his Lord-ship and Mrs. Marion Dal-rymple, containing tailzie of the lordship of *Rae,* and o-thers.	CAITHNESS and SUTHERLAND.

No	Vol.	Fol	Date of Tailzie	Date of Regist.	ENTAILERS NAMES and LANDS.	SHIRES.
					R, Continued.	
561	16	426	24 Jan. 1770	12 June 1771	RICKART (Mrs. Margaret) of Achnacant—Lands and eftate of *Achnacant*, and others.	ABERDEEN.
613	18	293	17 June 1751	9 July 1774	ROSS (George, Lord)—Lands and eftate of *Haukhead*, and others.	RENFREW & AYR.
623	18	430	1 Jan. 1688	10 Mar. 1775	ROTHES (Margaret, Countefs of)—Earldom of *Rothes*, and others.	FIFE, PERTH, KINCARDINE, FORFAR, and INVERNESS.
624	18	446	2 May 1775	23 June 1775	RUTHVEN (James, Lord)—Lands and eftate of *Forteviot*, and others.	PERTH.
661	20	1	14 Aug. 1771	14 Jan. 1779	RONALDSON (Andrew) of Blairhall—Lands and barony of *Blairhall*, and others.	PERTH and FIFE.
—	20	21	16 Apr. 1778	14 Jan. 1779	RONALDSON (faid Andrew)—Difpofition and affignation relative to the above entail.	PERTH and FIFE.
678	20	293	23 Apr. 1673	9 Mar. 1780	ROSEBERRY (Archibald, Earl of)—Tailzie by Sir Archibald Primrofe in his favour, of the lands and eftate of *Dumenay*, alias *Dalmeny*, and others.	LINLITHGOW.

I i

No.	Vol.	Fol.	Date of Tailzie.	Date of Regist.	ENTAILERS NAMES and LANDS.	SHIRE.
					R, *Continued.*	
698	21	125	30 Mar. & 9 April 1781	8 Aug. 1781	RUTHVEN (James, Lord) and his fon—Reftriction and ratification of the entail of their eftate of *Forteviot*, and others, N° 624.	PERTH.
705	21	219	20 Oct. 1781	15 Dec. 1781	RIDDICK (Thomas) of Flofk— Lands and eftate of *Flofk*, and others.	DUMFRIES.

No.	Vol.	Fol.	Date of Tailzie.	Date of Regift.	ENTAILERS NAMES and LANDS.	SHIRES.
					S.	
3	1	17	7 May 1686	15 July 1691	SCOTT (Sir William) of Harden—Lands and eftate of *Harden*.	SELKIRK.
14	1	164	29 May 1691	8 Dec. 1694	SCOTT (Hugh) of Gallafheills—Lands and eftate of *Gallafheills*.	SELKIRK.
29	2	66	20 May 1691	23 June 1697	STIRLING (William) of Law—Lands and eftate of *Law*, and others.	STIRLING.
30	2	74	1 Feb. 1697	28 July 1697	SCOTT (John) of Melleny——Lands and eftate of *Melleny*.	EDINBURGH.
40	2	202	14 June 1700	4 July 1700	SANDILANDS (James) of Crabfton—Lands and eftate of *Crabfton*.	ABERDEEN.
45	2	243	24 Apr. 1699	31 July 1700	SCOTT (John and Thomas) of Melleny—Lands and eftate of *Melleny*.	EDINBURGH.
46	2	258	22 Oct. 1700	12 Feb. 1701	STRATHALLAN (William, Vifcount of)—Lands and barony of *Cromlix*, and others.	PERTH.

No.	Vol.	Fol.	Date of Tailzie.	Date of Regist.	ENTAILERS NAMES and LANDS.	SHIRES.
					S, *Continued.*	
52	3	16	1 Mar. 1701	24 Feb. 1702	SHAW (Sir John) of Greenock—Lands and eſtate of *Greenock*, and others.	RENFREW.
63	3	133	18 Sept. 1703	27 Jan. 1704	SEATON (Sir Alexander) of Pitmeddon—Lands and eſtate of *Pitmeddon.*	ABERDEEN.
65	3	140	28 Feb. 1704	29 Feb. 1704	SANDILANDS (William) of Couſton—Lands and eſtate of *Couſton.*	LINLITHGOW.
84	3	373	11 Mar. 1706	6 June 1706	SALTON (William, Lord)——Lands and barony of *Philorth*, and others..	ABERDEEN.
88	3	411	11 Oct. 1706	8 Mar. 1707	STEWART (Francis) of Frankfield, and Roſs of Balnagowan—Lands and barony of *Balnagowan*, and others..	ROSS and SUTHERLAND.
93	4	47	29 Dec. 1705	1 Nov. 1707	SCOTT (Sir William) of Harden—Lands and barony of *Mertoune*, and others.	BERWICK and ROXBURGH..
101	4	132	8 April 1708	3 June 1709	SINCLAIR (John) of Ulbſter—Lands and barony of *Hoy*, and others.	CAITHNESS.

No.	Vol	Fol.	Date of Tailzie.	Date of Regist.	ENTAILERS NAMES and LANDS.	SHIRES.
					S, *Continued.*	
105	4	164	11 June 1703	23 Feb. 1710	STEVENSON (Sir Archibald) Doctor of Medicine—*His Houfes* *in Edinburgh.*	EDINBURGH.
112	4	221	18 Mar. 1702	20 Jan. 1711	SINCLAIR (Henry) of Carlourie —Lands and eftate of *Carlourie,* and others.	EDINBURGH.
126	4	367	4 Feb. 1713	21 July 1713	SINCLAIR (Matthew) of Herd-manfton, Doctor of Medicine —Lands and barony of *Herd-manflon,* and Mains thereof.	EDINBURGH.
138	5	92	6 Oct. 1704	25 June 1715	STEWART (John) of Blackhall —Lands and eftate of *Black-hall.*	No fhire mentioned.
146	5	144	15 Aug. 1716	3 July 1718	SINCLAIR (Henry, Lord)—— Lands and barony of *Ravenf-craig,* and others.	FIFE.
156	5	220	18 June 1719	18 July 1719	STEWART (John) of Phifgill— Lands of *Phifgill,* and others.	WIGTOUN.
160	5	253	4 Nov. 1664	26 Feb. 1720	STEWART (Sir James) of Stra-brock—Lands of *Strabrock,* and others.	LINLITHGOW.

K k

No.	Vol.	Fol.	Date of Tailzie.	Date of Regist.	ENTAILERS NAMES and LANDS.	SHIRES.
					S, *Continued.*	
161	5	259	31 May 1717	8 June 1720	STEWART (John) of Grantully—Lands and barony of *Grantully*, and others.	PERTH.
165	5	320	24 Aug. 1720	24 June 1721	SALMOND (Patrick) of Balquhatston—-Lands and estate of *Balquhatston*, and others.	STIRLING.
196	6	237	22 Feb. 1727	8 Dec. 1724	STAIR (John, Earl of)—Lands and baronies of *Stair*, and others.	WIGTOUN, AYR, LINLITHGOW, & EDINBURGH.
199	6	272	24 Oct. 1721	6 July 1725	SKENE (Major George) of Carraldston—Lands and estate of *Carraldston*, and others.	FORFAR.
235	7	188	23 Feb. 1714	7 June 1728	SINCLAIR (Sir John) of Stevenston—-Lands and barony of *Stevenston*, and others.	EDINBURGH.
270	8	199	22 July 1731	12 July 1732	STRANG (James) of Earnock—Lands of *Meikle Earnock*.	LANERK.
275	8	257	28 Mar. 1732	29 June 1733	SIVEWRIGHT (David) of Meggetland—Lands and barony of *Southhouse*.	EDINBURGH.

No.	Vol.	Fol.	Date of Tailzie.	Date of Regift	ENTAILERS NAMES and LANDS.	SHIRES.
					S, *Continued.*	
290	8	378	19 Apr. 1733	24 July 1734	SMITH (David) of Methven—Lands, lordfhip, and barony of *Methven.*	PERTH.
291	8	393	23 July 1734	25 July 1734	STEWART (James) of Camilla—Lands and barony of *Camilla.*	FIFE.
293	8	407	31 Jan. 1735	20 Feb. 1735	STRUTHERS (John) and Janet Hairfhaw—The lands and eftate of *Udftonhead* and *Carndufflaw.*	LANERK.
295	8	429	26 Mar. 1706	27 Feb. 1735	SMITH (Robert) portioner of Mallatfheugh—Lands of *Mallatfheugh,* and others.	RENFREW.
297	9	1	9 Mar. 1721	21 June 1735	SHAIRP (Thomas) of Houftoun—Lands and eftate of *Houftoun.*	LINLITHGOW.
305	9	59	11 June 1728	2 July 1736	SMOLLET (Sir James) of Bonhill—Tailzie, and deed of alteration and deftination relative thereto, of the lands and eftate of *Latroulbeg,* and others.	DUNBARTON.

No.	Vol.	Fol.	Date of Tailzie.	Date of Regift.	ENTAILERS NAMES *and* LANDS.	SHIRES.
					S, *Continued.*	
306	9	72	13 Apr. 1736	2 July 1736	SMOLLET (James) of Bonhill— Lands and eſtate of *Bonhill*, and others.	DUNBARTON.
313	9	167	23 May 1715	6 June 1738	STEWART (Captain John) of Dons—-Lands and eſtate of *Smiddiecroft, Kingcrown,* and others.	ABERDEEN.
314	9	172	3 May 1716	22 June 1738	SPREULL (John) of Miltoun— Lands and eſtate of *Cloberhill,* alias *Cardonhill,* and others.	DUNBARTON and LANERK.
321	9	283	21 May 1739	10 Nov. 1739	STAIR (John, Earl of)—Lands and eſtate of *Stair,* and others.	WIGTOUN, AYR, LINLITHGOW, EDINBURGH, and BERWICK.
370	11	51	5 Aug. 1746	11 Dec. 1746	SINCLAIR (John) of Sinclair— Barony of *Ravenſcraig.*	FIFE.
372	11	66	22 Jan. 1735	20 Dec. 1746	STEEDMAN (Helen) of Earnſide—Lands and eſtate of *Earnſides, North* and *South,* and others.	FIFE.

No.	Vol.	Fol.	Date of Tailzie.	Date of Regift.	ENTAILERS NAMES and LANDS.	SHIRES.
					S, *Continued.*	
378	11	136	31 Mar. 1747	17 Nov. 1747	STAIR (John, Earl of)—Lands and barony of *Stair*, *Maxton*, and others.	AYR, WIGTOUN, EDINBURGH, LINLITHGOW, and BERWICK.
393	11	382	14 July 1750	20 July 1750	SHAIRP (Thomas) of Houston —Lands and eftate of *Houfton-mains*, and others.	LINLITHGOW.
397	11	446	11 Aug. 1729	15 Nov. 1750	SCOTT (William) of Whitehaugh —Lands of *Whitehaugh*, and others.	ROXBURGH.
432	12	356	7 June 1755	31 July 1755	SHAIRP (Thomas) of Houftoun ——Lands of *Carriber*, and others.	LINLITHGOW.
441	12	465	20 Aug. 1756	8 Mar. 1757	SMOLLET (James) of Bonhill ——Lands of *Bonhill*, and others.	DUNBARTON.
447	13	65	29 June and 2 July 1757	9 Dec. 1757	SINCLAIR (John) of Stevenfton —Contract of excambion betwixt him and William, Lord Blantyre—*Six Acres of Land of Clerkington.*	EDINBURGH.

No.	Vol.	Fol.	Date of Tailzie.	Date of Regist.	ENTAILERS NAMES *and* LANDS.	SHIRES.
					S, Continued.	
463	13	256	31 May 1717	1 Mar. 1760	STEWART (John) of Grantul- ly—Nomination of heirs to fucceed him in his entailed e- ftate of *Grantully*, N° 161.	
477	14	25	14 Oct. 1762	23 Nov. 1762	SCOTT (David) of Scotftarvet— Barony of *Scotftarvet*, and o- ther eftates pertaining to him— And Additional deed relative thereto. *Nota.* Decreet of reduction of thefe two deeds by the Lords of Council and Seffion, dated 11th March 1773, (G. P. R. clerks.)	FIFE.
481	14	85	31 Oct. 1755	4 Feb. 1763	ST CLAIR (General James) of Sinclair—Lands and baronies of *Ravenfcraig, Dyfart, Rofline,* and others—And declaration relative thereto.	FIFE and EDIN- BURGH.
498	14	335	21 Aug. 1764	9 Mar. 1765	STEVENSON (Allan) copper- fmith in Glafgow—*Certain Te- nements of Land lying in the Burgh of Glafgow.*	LANERK.

No.	Vol.	Fol.	Date of Regift.	Date of Tailzie.	ENTAILERS NAMES and LANDS.	SHIRES.
					S, *Continued.*	
508	14	474	8 Aug. 1764	20 Feb. 1767	STEWART (James) of Killi-whinleck, and Mrs. Janet Stewart of Kildonan—Their eftates of *Killiwhinleck* and *Kildonan*, and others.	BUTE.
509	14	489	7 Nov. 1741	10 Mar. 1767	STEVENSON (William) of Nether Barbeth—Lands of *Nether Barbeth*.	AYR.
514	15	1	9 Dec. 1766	8 Dec. 1767	STEWART (Captain Keith)—Tailzie in his favour by the Earl of Galloway, of the lands of *Glafferton*, and others.	WIGTOUN.
522	15	250	23 Feb. 1768	26 Feb. 1768	SMOLLET (James) of Bonhill—Lands of *Drumfoddoch*, and others.	DUNBARTON.
543	16	90	19 Dec. 1768	6 Dec. 1769	SHARP (Matthew) of Hoddam—Lands and eftate of *Hoddam*, and others.	DUMFRIES and KIRKCUDBRIGHT.

No.	Vol.	Fol.	Date of Tailzie.	Date of Regift.	ENTAILERS NAMES and LANDS.	SHIRES.
					S, Continued.	
562	16	434	5 Oct. 1770	13June1771	STEWART (Captain Keith)—– Tailzie in his favour by the Earl of Galloway and Lord Garlies—Lands and farms of *Lagan* and *Claymodie*—And	WIGTOUN.
563	—	—	2 & 5 Mar. & 11June1771	13June1771	Deed of alteration relative thereto, and of the entail of lands of *Glafferton*.	
564	16	458	5 Oct. 1765	15June1771	STIRLING (Sir James) of Glorat—Lands of *Eafter* and *Wefter Glorats*, and others.	STIRLING.
567	16	491	28May1763	3 July 1771	STEWART (John) of Afcog, alias Murray of Blackbarony—Lands of *Afcogs*, and others.	BUTE & ARGYLE.
576	17	114	29Oct. 1771	17Jan. 1772	STEWART (Captain Keith)—– Tailzie in his favour by the Earl of Galloway and Lord Garlies, of lands of *Meiklehills*, part of the barony of *Glafferton.*	WIGTOUN.
589	17	351	3 Oct. 1767	1 Dec. 1772	STEWART (Walter) of Orchilbeg—Lands and eftate of *Orchilbeg*, and others.	PERTH.

No.	Vol.	Fol.	Date of Tailzie.	Date of Regist.	ENTAILERS NAMES and LANDS.	Suites.
					S, *Continued.*	
596	18	1	20May1719	30June1773	SCOTT (Sir William) of Thirleftane——Lands of *Boirhope, Thirleftane, Ramfcleugh,* and others.	SELKIRK.
599	18	53	2 & 3 Aug. 1773.	5 Aug. 1773	STEWART (Captain Keith) of Glafferton——Tailzie by him, with confent of John, Lord Garlies, of lands of *Glafferton, Claymoddie, Laggan,* and lands of *Meiklehills.*	WIGTOUN.
627	18	494	9 Feb. 1768	7 Dec. 1775	STEWART-HOME (David) of Argatty——Lands and barony of *Argatty,* and others.	PERTH.
656	19	467	9 May 1778	17June1778	STEWART (James) of Stewarthall—Lands and eftate of *Kilwhinleck,* and others.	BUTE and EDINBURGH.
676	20	258	9 Dec. 1779	17Feb. 1780	SPEIRS (Alexander) merchant in Glafgow—Lands and eftate of *Arkleton,* and others.	LANERK and RENFREW.

No.	Vol.	Fol.	Date of Tailzie.	Date of Regift.	ENTAILERS NAMES *and* LANDS.	SHIRE.
					, S, *Continued*.	
713	21	401	11 Jan. 1771	31 July 1782	SYDSERF (John) of Rucklaw, and Mrs. Martha Sydſerf—Eſtate of *Rucklaw*.	EDINBURGH.
717	21	469	13 Sept. 1780	16 Jan. 1783	SPEIRS (Alexander) of Elderſlie, merchant in Glaſgow—Lands and eſtate of *Culcruich, Provan-ſton, Cumming, Glens,* and others.	STIRLING.

No.	Vol.	Fol.	Date of Tailzie.	Date of Regift.	ENTAILERS NAMES *and* LANDS.	SHIRES.
					T.	
13	1	141	18 May 1694	8 Nov. 1694	TURNER (Robert) of Rofehill—Lands and eſtates of *Rofehill* and *Newark*, entailed by John Rofs of Rofehill.	ABERDEEN.
341	10	200	16 Dec. 1698	22 Dec. 1743	TARBET (George, Viſcount of)—Lands and eſtate of *Mey*, and others.	CAITHNESS & ROSS
364	10	142	26 July 1745	17 July 1749	TAYLOR (Samuel) in Aſhyburn—Lands and eſtate of *Drumboy*.	LANERK.
404	12	40	27 Dec. 1738	6 June 1752	TRENT (Dame Elizabeth) relict of Sir James Falconer of Pheſdo—Lands and eſtate of *Balmakettle*, and others.	KINCARDINE.
524	15	281	16 May 1760	18 June 1768	THOMSON (Alexander) advocate in Aberdeen—Lands and barony of *Banchory*, and others.	ABERDEEN and KINCARDINE.
553	16	265	6 Feb. 1764	28 July 1772	THOMSON (Robert) of Eaſter Fodderly, and Robert Dick, baillie of Jedburgh—Lands of *Eaſter Fodderly*.	ROXBURGH.

No.	Vol.	Fol.	Date of Tailzie.	Date of Regift.	ENTAILERS NAMES *and* LANDS.	SHIRES.
					T, *Continued.*	
574	17	57	12 Aug. 1771	13 Nov. 1771	TWEEDDALE (George, Marquis of)—-Lands and earldom of *Tweeddale*, and others.	EDINBURGH, BER-WICK, FIFE, and RENFREW.
634	19	133	5 Mar. 1776	7 Mar. 1776	TROTTER (Thomas) of Morton-hall—Lands of *Mortonhall*, and others.	EDINBURGH and BERWICK.
702	21	165	27 Jan. 1776	24 Nov. 1781	THOMSON (John) of Charleton —Lands and eſtate of *Charle-ton*, and others.	FIFE.

No.	Vol.	Fol.	Date of Tailzie	Date of Regift.	ENTAILERS NAMES and LANDS.	SHIRES.
					W.	
17	1	193	10 Sept 1695	6 & 7 Feb. 1696.	WILSON (George) of Plewlands —Two tailzies of the lands of *Plewlands.* Revocation of thefe, regiftered 28th February 1718.	LINLITHGOW.
34	2	119	27 May 1698	7 Jan. 1699	WAUCHOPE (Andrew) of Niddery—Lands and eftate of *Niddery*, and others.	EDINBURGH and ROXBURGH.
50	2	375	27 Oct. 1697	11 June 1701	WRIGHT (James) of Kerfie— Lands and eftate of *Kerfie*, and others.	STIRLING.
59	3	97	4 Oct. 1682	21 July 1703	WATSONS (David and James) of Sauchton—Lands and eftate of *Sauchton.*	EDINBURGH.
85	3	385	1 April 1706	13 June 1706	WRIGHT (Alexander) merchant, burgefs of Edinburgh-—*Some Houfes lying in Canongatehead of Edinburgh*, entailed by James Syme, flater in Edinburgh, and Patrick Simpfon, flater in Canongate.	EDINBURGH.

N n

No.	Vol.	Fol.	Date of Tailzie.	Date of Regist.	ENTAILERS NAMES and LANDS.	SHIRES.
					W, *Continued.*	
89	3	440	9 Nov. 1702	14 Mar. 1707	WILLIAMSON (James) of Cardrouna—Lands of *Cardrouna*, and others.	PEEBLES.
144	5	142	2 Feb. 1703	28 Feb. 1718	WILSON (George) of Plewlands—Difcharge and renunciation of the entail of *Plewlands.*	LINLITHGOW.
149	5	175	4 Jan. 1718	27 Nov. 1718	WISCHART (Sir George) of Cliftonhall—Lands and eftate of *Auldlifton*, and others.	EDINBURGH and LINLITHGOW.
231	7	149	23 Mar. 1725	25 July 1727	WODDROP (John) of Wefthorn—Lands and eftate of *Wefter Albeth,* and others.	LANERK.
243	7	269	12 Dec. 1728	22 Jan. 1729	WATT (James) brewer in Orchardfield—Lands of *Livingfton's-Yards.*	EDINBURGH.
259	8	72	11 Apr. 1729	14 Jan. 1731	WIGHTMAN (John) of Mauldflie—Lands and eftate of *Mauldflie*, and others—And Declaration relative thereto.	EDINBURGH.

No.	Vol.	Fol.	Date of Tailzie	Date of Regift.	ENTAILERS NAMES and LANDS.	SHIRES.
					W, *Continued.*	
338	10	115	16Sept.1742	6 Nov. 1742	WELSH (Alexander) of Scarr— Lands and eftate of *Barfkeoch*, and others.	KIRKCUDBRIGHT and DUMFRIES.
391	11	363	24June1741	23Feb. 1750	WIGTON (John, Earl of)—— Lands, lordfhip and barony of *Cumbernauld*, and others.	LANERK, STIRLING, PEEBLES, SELKIRK, and HADDINGTON.
399	12	1	29May1751	11June1751	WELLWOOD (Henry) of Garvock—-Lands and eftate of *Garvock*, and others.	FIFE.
425	12	278	2 July 1753	15Feb. 1755	WELLWOOD (Henry) of Garvock—-Lands and eftate of *Tillibole*.	FIFE.
506	14	453	31July 1766	6 Aug. 1766	WEDDERBURN (Grizel) of Wedderburn—Lands and eftate of *Wedderburn*.	FORFAR.
586	17	307	9 Jan. 1772	22July 1772	WALLACE (William) of Blacklaw—Lands and mailling of *Blacklaw*.	AYR.

No.	Vol.	Fol.	Date of Tailzie.	Date of Regift.	ENTAILERS NAMES *and* LANDS.	SHIRES.
					W, *Continued.*	
562	20	27	9 April 1778	21 Jan. 1779	WATSON (Alexander) of Turin—Lands and eftate of *Over* and *Nether Turins,* and others.	FORFAR.
597	21	123	5 July 1781	19 July 1781	WATSON (faid Alexander) of Turin—Revocation by him of the above tailzie of his lands of *Over* and *Nether Turins,* and others.	FORFAR.

No.	Vol.	Fol.	Date of Tailzie.	Date of Regist.	ENTAILERS NAMES and LANDS.	SHIRES.
					Y.	
267	8	171	5 June 1732	8 June 1732	YEOMAN (George) of Murie—Lands and barony of Murie-mains.	PERTH.
274	8	250	21 July 1732	27 Jan. 1733	YEOMAN (George) of Murie—Lands and barony of Murie, and others.	PERTH.
457	13	188	7 May 1754	1 Mar. 1759	YOUNG (John) taylor, burgefs of Edinburgh——Lands and Mains of Humbie.	EDINBURGH.
458	13	195	29 May 1754	1 Mar. 1759	YOUNG (faid John) taylor, burgefs of Edinburgh—Subjects about Collington.	EDINBURGH.
—	13	201	1 May 1758	1 Mar. 1759	YOUNG (faid John)—Confent and revocation by him of his tailzie.	EDINBURGH.
687	20	414	21 Nov. 1772	22 Nov. 1780	YOUNG (Harry) of Warrock—Lands of Eafter and Wefter Mains of Cleifh, Eafter and Wefter Borland of Cleifh, and others.	KINROSS.

[156]

२

A P P E N D I X,

CONTAINING

ALL THE ENTAILS RECORDED

Since the foregoing INDEX was printed, to 4th February 1784.

No.	Vol.	Fol	Date of Tailzie.	Date of Regift.	ENTAILERS NAMES and LANDS.	SHIRES.
					A.	
729	22	90	12 May 1783	9 Aug. 1783	ABERCROMBY (Mrs. Mary) widow of General James Abercromby of Glaſſa, and his other Truſtees—Lands of *Coynoch* and *Little Cocklaw*, in favour of William Abercromby of Glaſſa.	ABERDEEN.
					B.	
736	22	208	26 Apr. 1783	4 Feb. 1784	BARCLAY (Robert) of Capilrig, writer in Glaſgow—— Lands and eſtate of *Capilrig* and others, in favour of Miſs Mary Anderſon and the heirs whomſoever of her body, whom failing, to William Muir of Caldwell and his heirs-mail, &c.	RENFREW.

No.	Vol.	Fol.	Date of Tailzie.	Date of. Regist.	ENTAILERS NAMES and LANDS.	SHIRES.
					D.	
724	22	28	13Mar.1783	10July 1783	DUFF (Robert) of Fettereſſo, Vice-Admiral of the Red Squadron of his Majeſty's Fleet—Lands and eſtates of *Fettereſſo* and *Logie.*	KINCARDINE and ABERDEEN.
737	22	—	16July1783	4 Feb. 1784	DAVID (Lord Viſcount) of Stormont, William, Earl Mansfield, and George Roſs of Cromarty, truſtees of the deceaſed John, Earl of Dunmore ——Tailzie by them of lands and barony of *Elphinſtone* and others, in favour of John, now Earl of Dunmore.	STIRLING, PERTH, and ARGYLE.
					F.	
723	22	20	22June1781	9 July 1783	FLEMING (John) of Nook—Lands of *Nook,* with the pertinents.	LANERK.
					G.	
730	22	92	6 Aug. 1783	15Nov.1783	GLASFORD (John) of Dougalſton——Lands and eſtate of *Dougalſton* and others.	STIRLING and DUNBARTON.

No.	Vol.	Fol.	Date of Tailzie.	Date of Regift.	ENTAILERS NAMES *and* LANDS.	S H I R E S.
					M.	
722	22	1	4 Dec. 1781	17 June 1783	MARCHMONT (Hugh, Earl of) —His *lands, lordſhip, barony, mills, teinds, rights of patronage,* and others, lying within the ſhires of	BERWICK, HADDINGTON, and EDINBURGH.
725	22	43	5 Dec. 1771	19 July 1783	M'ARTHUR (John) of Miltoun —Lands and eſtate of *Miltoun* and others;	ARGYLE.
					As alſo,	
726	22	54	28 Sep. 1772	19 July 1783	RATIFICATION of ſaid deed of Tailzie, by Mrs. Mary Sandilands, relict of the ſaid John M'Arthur of Miltown;	
					And,	
727	22	58	17 July 1783	19 July 1783	M'ARTHUR - STEWART (Archibald) of Aſcog, ſon of the ſaid John M'Arthur of Miltoun——Lands and eſtate of *Drumfin* and others.	ARGYLE.

No.	Vol.	Fol.	Date of Tailzie.	Date of Regist.	INTAILLERS NAMES and LANDS.	Shires.
					M,—*continued.*	
730	22	70	16June1783	31July1783	BARCLAY-MAITLAND (Charles) of Tillycoultry—— Lands and barony of *Tillycoultry* and others, in favour of James Bruce, formerly Car- ſtairs, ſon of the deceaſed James Bruce-Carſtairs of Kin- roſs.	CLACKMANNAN.
731	22	114	18June1783	26Nov.1783	MAXWELL (David) of Cardo- neſs and others.	KIRKCUDBRIGHT.
732	22	128	17Aug.1781	3 Dec. 1783	MUIR (George) of Caffincarrie, principal clerk of Juſticiary— Lands and eſtate of *Caffincarrie,* and others;	DUMFRIES, WIG- TOUN, and Stew- artry of KIRKCUD- BRIGHT.
					And,	
732	22	147	19June1783	3 Dec. 1783	DEED OF REVOCATION of the foreſaid tailzie by Mr. Muir, in ſo far only as concerns Lieutenant Colonel Grainger Muir, one of the ſubſtitutes.	
733	22	150	17June1783	3 Dec. 1783	MUIR (the ſaid George)—Lands of *Cuill,* and others.	KIRKCUDBRIGHT.

No	Vol.	Fol.	Date of Tailzie	Date of Regist.	ENTAILERS NAMES and LANDS.	SHIRE.
					M,—*continued.*	
734	22	1698	July 1783	18 Dec. 1783	MUNRO (Sir George) of Pointz-field, with consent of Lady Mary Munro his wife—Lands of *Ardoch* and others.	CROMARTY and SUTHERLAND.
					S.	
735	22	1875	Nov. 1771	20 Dec. 1783	STIRLING (Archibald) of Keir —Lands and barony of *Keir,* and others.	PERTH, STIRLING, and LANERK.

F   I   N   I   S.

www.ingramcontent.com/pod-product-compliance
Lightning Source LLC
Chambersburg PA
CBHW020555270326
41927CB00006B/857